"Don't give your client answers - ̱ ....
"Space to See Reality," Carole Griggs explains clearly and simply how we can meet more authentically when we go beyond identification with our conceptual minds. Therapists, teachers, and healers of all kinds will benefit from this fresh new perspective on how profound change happens when our egos get out of the way. An important book that begins a long overdue conversation between coaching and non-dual spirituality."

Jeff Foster, author of *The Deepest Acceptance*

"Over the past fifty years, I have been exploring my own level of consciousness and applying it to my teachings, private practice, workshops, and life. So it is exhilarating to have one of our graduates write a book in an area that is crucial to the evolution of the planet, if not to our very existence. It is not only essential but timely for the coaching profession that we introduce the spiritual dimension into counseling, psychotherapy and coaching. Carole's book offers a clear and workable guide for this evolution to take place. I strongly recommend it to all coaches, no matter what area they specialize in."

Irv S. Katz, Ph.D., renowned psychologist and Chancellor of International University of Professional Studies

"It is so refreshing to find a Life Coach who is offering guidance to a client about Life as it really as, as opposed to life how it APPEARS. There is presently a monumental shift arising in human consciousness shown by the increasing number if people who are seeking to find out who they really are at Source. The old model of a therapist aiding the client in making themselves 'better' combined with great attention on goal-setting, is being superseded by the deepest desire from people to simply 'come home'. Carole Griggs has identified this need by the client to discover their inner Being, and how essential it is for the coach to know Oneself AS pure conscious awareness in order to allow this to be experienced by the client, as demonstrated in this quote from her book: ""Clearly it's important what the coach can do, but it's more important how he or she is being" (Silsbee, 2008, p. xii). A coach's recognition of "True Essence" as who one really is, directly influences and correlates to how he or she shows up for a client."

Carole expresses so beautifully and clearly how crucial it is for the Coach to be coming from Presence themselves so that they can 'hold the space' for the client's True nature to be revealed.

This book is a truly excellent and comprehensive guide for anyone who is capable and passionate enough about entering into relationships with clients where the focus is on the Absolute Self rather than the imagined, illusory sense of identity".

Mandi Solk, author of *The Joy of No Self,* and Self-Enquiry teacher based in Yorkshire, England

"Philosopher, Tielhard de Chardin once proclaimed that humans are not physical beings having a spiritual experience. Rather we "are spiritual beings having a physical experience." If that is true, then Dr. Carole Griggs has presented an exceptionally useful model for professional coaches to use when coaching persons. Her book, "Space to See Reality: A New Model for Professional Coaches" offers practical tips, questions and responses for coaches to explore the spiritual aspects of a client's life. It is a must read for anyone interested in assisting others to discover and explore their lives as spiritual beings."

Lloyd J. Thomas, Ph.D. Certified Psychologist and co-author of *"Total Life Coaching: 50+ Life Lessons, Skills, and Techniques to Enhance Your Practice ...and Your Life."*

SPACE TO SEE REALITY

A New Model for Professional Coaches

"What you are looking for is

what is looking."

CAROLE GRIGGS, PH.D.

Cover Image © Dr. Cliff Oliver
Cover Design by Kane Luong
Author photo © Victor Alan
Editor: Sangeet Duchane

Dedicated to Life.

CONTENTS

Acknowledgments

Preface

Part I: EXPLORING THE PREMISE

Introduction

Background Information

The Purpose of this Work

1   Exploring "Me" and the Ground of Being

2   Density and Transparency with Clients

Part II: PERMEATING ELEMENTS

3   Joining or Recognizing Sameness/Oneness

4   Fully Present

5   Radical Sincerity

6   Trusting Life

Conclusion

Potential Barriers

References

Appendix A

ACKNOWLEDGMENTS

With love and deep gratitude:
John and Sally Griggs
Susan Graham
Chelsea Reede
Jeff Foster
Lloyd Thomas
Peggy Webb

.

PREFACE

This book was originally written as part of a dissertation for a Doctorate degree in Professional Coaching and Human Development. The Background Information (Literature Review) has been condensed from its' original form, to offer interested readers insight into some of the history and research involved in the completion of this work. The Background Information provides a solid premise and sequential foundation for the chapters following; however, for those not interested in the history and research this is built upon, simply begin at Chapter One. Although the focus and research is primarily geared towards professional coaches, herein is a model that is relevant to therapists, nurses, doctors, teachers, counselors, and anyone that works one-on-one in the healing and helping profession that support others in getting unstuck. The target population for whom this model will likely serve best are primarily professionals with some prior experience with Consciousness, Awareness, Mindfulness, Stillness, et cetera, and who might find this model easier to understand and utilize.

The elements of this model are based on the premise of seeing life undivided. This in and of itself is a foundational approach/perspective that is yet to be traversed in coaching literature. It is potentially in closer alignment with practitioners less interested in managing, changing, fixing, goal setting, et cetera. The elements herein transcend many traditional aspects of coaching models, and thus may not feel comprehensively congruent with other professional coaching models or current approaches.

Part I

EXPLORING THE PREMISE

"What you are looking for is what is looking."
Saint Francis of Assisi (c. 1181–1226)

CAROLE GRIGGS, PH.D.

INTRODUCTION

In front of you the clouds parade by, your thoughts parade by, bodily sensations parade by, and you are none of them. You are the vast expanse of freedom through which all these objects come and go. You are an opening, a clearing, an Emptiness, a vast spaciousness, in which all these objects come and go. (Wilber, 2004, p. 15)

Transformation happens when people are seen as the Essence of who they truly are. A fundamental shift in identification, from the conceptual, mind-generated "personal self," to the ground of being, has the capacity to expand transformative possibilities of the coaching client as well as the field of coaching.

The idea that there is a "self"—separate and special and in charge of running "my" life—is purely an innocent mistake. It is simply a misunderstanding that there is some entity called "me" that exists. It is simply not true. As in, not true at all. This fundamental misunderstanding is the bedrock of all human turmoil and suffering. Through investigation, it appears that most current coaching literature is founded on this false premise. Most current coaching literature attempts to "make a better me" in some manner, which often perpetuates stuckness and struggle. Why continue to rearrange that which is unreal?

Current coaching literature thoroughly describes traditional and tangible skill-sets (Askew & Carnell, 2011; Cashman, 1998; Johnson& Eaton, 2001). In current coaching literature (Hargrove, 1999; Lasley, Kellogg, Michaels, & Brown, 2011; Schaik, 2012), the foundation for one's identity is primarily based on mental concepts, beliefs, and images. Current coaching texts and many ideological systems tend to stop short; they tend to stop at describing a "mature self." Since 550 B.C. however, ancient and contemporary literature has written about a "ground of being"—that which is beyond the conceptual mind—as the foundation for one's identity or increased awareness of who I am. Indeed, most of humanity derives identification of "the self" from the limited perspective of the conceptual mind. Such identification creates a false "personal sense" of me, which is nothing more than a conglomeration of thoughts, beliefs, and ideas bundled together to create one's personal identity called, "myself." This identification as a separate "self," leads individuals to attempt to manage, adjust, refine, remove, or change these illusory images of "the self." Yet as Ramana Maharshi once said, "There is no use removing doubts one by one. If we clear one doubt, another doubt will arise and there will be no end of doubts. But, if by seeking the doubter, the doubter is found to be really non-existent, then all doubts will cease" (Greenblatt, 2002, p. 109). This entity known as "me," simply doesn't exist. So why attempt to resolve or enhance that which is unreal?

I have yet to find coaching literature that clearly writes about coaching from the ground of being, which exists beyond the personal, mind-generated story of oneself; beyond the thinking-, learning-, conceptual-mind where the True Self exists (Wilber, 2007). I have not found coaching literature that specifically addresses coaching from beyond the thoughts, ideas, and stories of conditioned thinking, toward a timeless, unchanging, and formless essence. I have also not found coaching literature written specifically about the intangible elements that arise from this timeless ground of being perspective, and the impact this can have. This book examines ancient and contemporary literature in a way that offers an alternative premise for professional coaching. Adyashanti, a spiritual teacher based in northern California, shares:

> There's something deeper going on here; there's a possibility of looking at image in a whole new way, from an entirely different vantage point. Allow yourself to see that your self-image is just an image—not reality, not the truth, not who we really are. (Adyashanti, 2011, p. 21)

Herein is a new model for professional coaches, called, *Space to See Reality: A New Model for Professional Coaches.* This model will include elaboration on four intangible elements that are the natural emanation of this Ground of Being. It will describe the value of each element offering comprehensive examples, exercises, and tangible tools for practical implementation into the practice of professional coaching.

BACKGROUND INFORMATION

The coaching market is filled with coaching handbooks, models, manuals, and courses that cover traditional and tangible skill-sets. Almost all of these texts offer some form of advice about the making of a "better me" (Osteen, 2007). Some attend to goal-setting and goal achieving (Lasley, Kellogg, Michaels, & Brown, 2011). Others recommend developing purpose (Belf, 2002). Still others suggest visualization and imagery (Lasley, 2010). While all of these developmental activities have their place in coaching, they all lack a fundamental ingredient: the identification with the very Ground of Being; the absence of my "self."

Spiritual teacher, Karen Richards, writes about the concept of the ground of being, when she states, "Until you recognize what is ultimately true and essentially make that the priority in life, you will always view problems through the lens of experience – rather than the ground of experience" (Richards, 2013). Shifting one's perspective from the lens of self to the ground of experience has immense impact on a coach-client relationship and is, therefore, an invitation for comprehensive exploration.

Humanistic psychology (Maslow, 1968), transpersonal psychology (Hart, Nelson, & Puhakka, 2000; Wilber, 2000), existential psychology (Boadella, 1998; Valle, King, & Halling, 1989), consciousness studies (Forman, 1998; Rothberg, 1994), philosophical concepts (Levinas, 1969; Watts, 1975) and spiritual traditions (Mitchell, 1998; Tolle, 1999), all play a role in any fundamental shift in one's identity within a coach-client relationship. This book provides an examination of these texts that recognize the relevance of the personal self, while at the same time, points to something beyond. It suggests a fundamental shift of one's identification: from the thoughts, ideas, and stories of conditioned thinking to one's timeless, unchanging, and formless essence.

Behaviorism and psychoanalysis are the two main schools of traditional psychology, developed in the middle of the 20th century (Grof, 2008). According to the Institute of Transpersonal Psychology (a private graduate school founded in 1975), traditional psychology is focused on human behavior, with a linear spectrum of severe dysfunction on one end and "normal," healthy behavior on the other end. Psychoanalysis and behaviorism were the primary focus of the time, with their foundations stemming from the notion of examining and fixing the self.

Humanistic psychology (now called positive psychology) was developed in the 1950s, primarily by Abraham Maslow and Carl Rogers. These developments were prompted by the "disregard for consciousness and introspection," and an overemphasis on behavior and dysfunction (Grof, 2008). Both Maslow's and Rogers' work emphasized the importance of focusing on the clients' present experience, rather than emphasizing the past or future. Maslow wrote, "What is necessary to change a person is to change his awareness of himself" (Stephens, 1972, p. 21). Although Maslow's recognition of self-awareness and identification as necessary for human development surfaced at this time, humanistic studies primarily stayed within the functional realm of a separate self.

According to Bettina Bergo (2005) in *Existence and Existents*, French existential philosopher Emmanuel Levinas speaks of "there is" as the ground of *Being"* (p. 42). Levinas describes this Being, or "there is," as not "nothing," but as "a field without master," which, "turns into the horror and dissolution of our 'me.'" In *Totality and Infinity: An Essay on Exteriority*, Levinas refers to Being as "Other" and "To meet the Other is to have the idea of Infinity" (p. 51).

In the mid-1960s, the concepts of transpersonal psychology emerged. This new psychology was primarily pioneered by Maslow, Carl Jung, Ken Wilber, and Stanislav Grof. Grof explains that transpersonal psychology, "honors the entire spectrum of human experience, including various non-ordinary states of consciousness" (Grof, 2008, p. 3). The name itself is said to have been derived from the word, "transhumanistic," which meant, "reaching beyond humanistic concerns" (p. 3). Transpersonal psychology acknowledged that attention beyond the personal self was the primary means of personal identification. In his book, *The Simple Feeling of Being: Embracing Your True Nature*, Ken Wilber, pioneering transpersonal psychologist and writer, speaks in great detail about the ground of being (Wilber, 2004). On the back cover of this book, Wilber brings the "ground of being" to the fore when he writes:

As you look deeply into your own awareness, and relax the self-contraction, and dissolve into the empty ground of your own primordial experience, the simple feeling of Being—right now, right here—is it not obvious all at once? Were you not present from the start? Did you not have a hand to play in all that was to follow? Did not the dream itself begin when you got bored with being God? Was it not fun to get lost in the productions of your own wondrous imagination, and pretend it all was other? Did you not write this book, and countless others like it, simply to remind you who you are?" (Wilber, 2004)

According to Shambhala Publications, Wilber is considered not only a pioneer of transpersonal psychology, but also a spiritual luminary of our time (Wilber, 2004). Although this ground of being notion came to fruition through the field of transpersonal psychology, within the past half century; saints, sages, and various spiritual "leaders" have been referring to the ground of being as existing throughout human history.

This "empty ground . . . simple feeling of Being" that Wilber refers to on the back cover of his 2004 book, is the very essence that spiritual teachers have been writing and speaking about at least since 550 BC. Lau-tzu, thought to be an older contemporary of Confucius (551–479 BC), is the author of the *Tao Te Ching*, which is known to be "one of the wonders of the world" (Mitchell, 1998, p. vii). In the 25th chapter of Stephen Mitchell's 1998 translation of the Tao, Lau-tzu points to this ground of being when he writes:

"There was something formless and perfect
Before the universe was born
It is serene. Empty
Solitary. Unchanging.
Infinite. Eternally present.
It is the mother of the universe.
I call it the Tao." (p. 25)

Modern spiritual teacher, Adyashanti, similarly defines this ground of being in an article he wrote, entitled, "The Immensity of

Solitude" (Adyashanti, 2012c). He wrote:

> In that solitude all ideas and images are left behind, and we can intuitively orient ourselves toward the unborn and uncreated ground of being. In that ground we find our true being; and in the same manner in which our being is uncreated, it is also undying. Therefore, all that we will ever be or can be is found in our solitude (within ourselves) and is timelessly present in its fullness and completeness, now and eternally. (p. 1)

Current coaching texts and most psychological and philosophical studies tend to stop at a "mature self" as the premise of one's identity. Coaching from the premise of a mature self is dramatically different than what many of the great luminaries call the "True Self," or the ground of being. A large body of literature already examines the subject of "who I am" as the ground of being. Sri Nisargadatta Maharaj refers to the timeless essence as, "Awareness" (Frydman, M., & Dikshit, S. S, 1999), Eckhart Tolle; "consciousness" (1999), Levinas; "Other" (1969), Lau-tzu; the "Tao" or "The Way" (550 BC), Gangaji, "limitless being" (2007), John Welwood, "Presence" (2000), and Ken Wilber, "Emptiness," "Big Mind," and "True Self" (2004, 2007). Nevertheless, according to my investigation, I have not found any coaching literature today that comprehensively studies the interconnected relationship between these ancient and contemporary teachings and their influence in the professional coaching environment. Such a relationship could dramatically enrich the current body of professional coaching literature, of which I have yet to find that specifically addresses coaching from beyond the thinking-, conceptual-mind.

This spaciousness spoken of here is found in some professional coaching literature, typically under a chapter entitled "spirituality."

However, the way in which it is currently written about is boldly different than what is presented here. The literature that does speak of coaching and these elements, speaks from an entirely different premise; a premise stemming from a separate "me" that "uses" Spirit as a means to enhance, change, create, et cetera. For example, in Teri-E. Belf's book, *Coaching with Spirit*, she explains that, "The dual purpose of *Coaching with Spirit* is to increase coaches' awareness of the part Spirit plays in their interactions with clients and to enhance coaching effectiveness by welcoming and integrating Spirit into coaching meetings" (2002, p. xvii). This assumes a separate me "using" something called Spirit, from a place of division. In the way it will be presented here, spirituality, Life, whatever term preferred, is not a separate dimension that is inserted and applied like a strategy or technique. This aspect is simply the foundation, the ground from which all rises, and is. There is no "I" that "uses" Spirit, uses Presence, uses anything. There is simply no such entity called "me" that exists to "use" what you are.

In *Presence-Based Coaching*, Silsbee explores, "how to develop and use presence to evoke change in others as well as in yourself" (2008, p. 3). This presupposes an individual separate self that "uses Presence" with intent and purpose to benefit "me" and "you," which instantly suggests a divide. In this new model, we are going to explore how there really is no I to use Presence or Spirit. From this space there is no need for techniques, strategies, or advanced moves to use Being, the very essence of what you are. Peeling away false images and beliefs that make up this separate me, and seeing life as it actually is, can begin to reveal this limitless, transparent nature that you are. As Nirmala points to in *Nothing Personal*, "All of our suffering, all of our struggle, and all of our problems relate back to one simple misunderstanding: the belief that anything is separate from anything else and, particularly, the belief that we are separate entities" (2007, p. 59). This book explores a fundamental shift in coaching in a way that has yet to be written about in the coaching profession. Presented here is a drastic shift from perceived separation, to movement from/as unity, and the value of coaching from that unified field of vast transparency, also known as Reality.

Within this investigation, I also did not find coaching literature written specifically on the intangible elements that arise from vast spaciousness (Wilber, 2004). Joining or Recognizing Sameness-Oneness; Fully Present; Radical Sincerity; and Don't Know are four intangible elements that are the natural emanation of this ground of being (refer to following pages for details). Some current coaching literature (Belf, 2002; Lasley, 2010; Silsbee, 2008) touches on a few aspects of these elements as "being present," "acceptance," "listening," or "authenticity." However, I haven't found any writings about these topics from the foundation and perspective that is beyond the self. As contemporary spiritual teacher, Mooji, says, "If we give remedies along the way, it is perpetuating a belief in a self that doesn't really exist. It is looking for medicine for a ghost. Everybody believes this story" (Mooji, 2011). This book takes a profound look at the coach-client relationship and environment from a viewpoint other than the illusive self . . . but from the timeless, unborn, Ground of Being.

It is essential to begin to fill the gap between the premise of current coaching literature, and the foundation derived from ancient and contemporary literature. Shifting into this latter alternative premise also presents elements not yet explored in professional coaching. There is also a need to explore the intangible elements that arise from this shift in perspective within the coaching environment, and give notice to the impact they can have.

THE PURPOSE OF THIS WORK

a) Suggest and describe a paradigm shift from current professional coaching approaches, to an alternative premise rooted in ancient and contemporary studies.

b) Introduce four intangible elements that arise in a coach-client environment from this shift in perspective: Joining or Recognizing Sameness-Oneness; Fully Present; Radical Sincerity; and Don't Know.

c) Explain the deep relevance, value, and impact these elements can have within the coaching environment.

d) Provide coaches with practical examples, exercises, and tools for practice and implementation for him or herself and with their clients.

Within this work, I suggest and describe a paradigm shift from current professional coaching approaches, to an alternative premise rooted in ancient and contemporary studies. According to my investigation, the current premise for coaching literature is based on personal identification with ideas, beliefs, and thoughts as the basis of who I am. However, the alternative perspective points to, and is based upon, the fundamental shift of one's identification from the thoughts, ideas, and stories of conditioned thinking as the basis of who I am, to one's identity as a timeless, unchanging, and formless Essence.

Since there appears to be an absence of coaching literature that writes specifically about coaching from beyond the thinking-, conceptual-mind, herein will be a new model with a clear description of this shift in identification and the impact this way of being and "seeing" can have in a coach-client relationship. Laske (2003) uses the term "Structure of Interpretation," which is a "System of interrelated developmental and behavioral variables that determine how the world shows up for the client" (p. 54). According to Laske, how the world appears for somebody always limits his or her options. If this is true, a shift in how the coach shows up—how he or she identifies himself or herself—has the potential to alter the possibilities available to the client. Instead of just examining what a coach says or does, the focus becomes how a coach is being. In effect, a coach's way of identification influences what he or she does, what is said, and how things are seen. "Clearly it's important what the coach can do, but it's more important how he or she is *being*" (Silsbee, 2008, p. xii).

At the 2013 *Science and Nonduality Conference* in San Jose, CA, Stanslov Grof, a psychologist and psychiatrist with more than fifty years' experience researching the healing and transformative potential of non-ordinary states of consciousness, shares insights on the importance beyond the particular (therapist/coach) technique, and emphasis towards what he calls the "quality of human interaction."

During his talk, entitled, *Revision and Re-Enchantment of Psychology: Legacy from Half Century of Consciousness Research*, Grof shares insights on studies that show there is no real statistical difference in therapy results from one (psychology) school offering better results than another, and if anything, the results are inside of the schools based on something—the actual interaction itself—that the therapist doesn't usually think about. Each school comes with a different explanation for client "problems," along with different techniques to utilize. Grof says it's like "flipping a coin" in deciding which explanation and what technique will be most beneficial. Grof opens this deeper when he explains, "There are better therapists and not so good therapists. Some of these studies show what really works in psychotherapy is something that therapists don't really think about and it's very difficult to put into scientific language, something called the quality of human encounter between the therapist and the client, or the feeling of the client of being unconditionally accepted by another human being frequently for the first time in their life; effectiveness of this kind." With this, Grof introduces what he terms, "the holotropic alternative," describing this alternative as one that "mobilizes self-healing potential." In Grof's 2007 article entitled, *Holotropic Experiences and Their Healing and Heuristic Potential*, he explains and defines holotropic as, "the composite word literally means oriented toward wholeness" (p. 1). Grof says that it is in this "holotropic state," when we are orientated towards wholeness, "we become more like midwives, not the fixers with brilliant insights and interpretations (which will be different depending on the school). . . you simply support what is happening. . . we believe there is a deeper intelligence that is operating in these states". How a coach (or therapist) shows up, how he or she is "being," can and quite often does have significant impact in a client's process.

The coach's recognition of "True Essence" as who one really is—directly influences and correlates to how he or she shows up for a client. This alternative way of identification offers an environment ripe for deep opening, authentic inquiry, raw vulnerability, profound clarity, and an inviting space for true liberation from a limited sense of personal identity.

Since I have not found any current coaching literature that writes specifically about coaching from beyond the thinking-, conceptual-mind; I have also not found coaching literature written specifically on the intangible elements that arise from timeless space. Outlined and described herein are four intangible elements that permeate the substance of the ground of being, also referred to as Vast Space. Joining or Recognizing Sameness-Oneness; Fully Present; Radical Sincerity; and Don't Know are four intangible elements that are the natural emanation of this mysterious ground of being, or as Wilber (2004) calls it, Suchness of Emptiness. The mysterious Suchness of Vast Space is what many of the saints, sages, philosophers, and mystics (as referenced earlier) have pointed to over the years. Evered and Selman (1987) open the door for a deeper investigation to the field of coaching when they claim that, "coaching provides the possibility of dealing with what is not seen, or even seeable, from the prevailing paradigm" (p. 27). Evered and Selman briefly touch into the very essence of the work that is presented herein; the investigation of the relevance, value, and impact of the intangible aspects that exist within a coach-client space.

Below is a brief table, comparing the basis of this work to the current coaching literature.

Space to See Reality Coaching Model	Current Coaching Literature
I am that which sees the me	I am the me
See through me	Construct, build, create a "better me"
Transparent	Solidify beliefs/thoughts/certainty
Heart	Head: intellectual, rational, logical
Un-Learn	Learn: Educate, gain knowledge
Here/present	Past/Future
Uncompromised attention	Planning, thinking, strategizing
Radical Acceptance	Fix/change/make different/save
One - united	You/Me: separate
Sameness	Hierarchy, differences
Sincerity, Authenticity, Realness	Role-playing, connecting through images of me
Don't Know	Development towards more knowing
Trust Life	Agenda, goals, excessive planning, reliant on personal me

Table 1

Space to See Reality Coaching vs. Current Coaching Literature

The "personal self," although illusory and subjective, is not ignored, suppressed, or denied. This would be what Robert Masters refers to as "spiritual bypassing," a "devaluation of the personal relative to the spiritual" (2010, p. 2). The "starting point," if you will, is beyond the conceptual identity of a separate self, and concurrently acknowledges and embraces the "personal" aspects of the physical and psychological, birthed from Vast Space. In the video, *What is Awakening,* Mooji clarifies:

> There continues to be a kind of maturing, a kind of evolving; but simultaneously against a background of unchanging Awareness. There isn't a person becoming better and better. What is happening is that the person is slowly vanishing. And what remains is just the dynamic existence, the pure existence without the psychological projection that comes from the idea of a person. (2013)

The key aspect in giving recognition to this evolving, maturing, disappearing self, is seeing from (as), the ground of being, rather than as the illusive story of me. The ground of being gives rise to the four elements mentioned above and discussed below.

Joining or Recognizing Sameness-Oneness

When the coach sees a client from Presence, as Presence, it invites the client to drop out of identification with the mind, and as spaciousness itself. This is simply Life recognizing itself in another as itself. There is no longer separation, no longer a me and a you (a coach and a client); simply a continuum. Transformation happens when clients are genuinely seen, heard, understood, and recognized as the very Essence of who they truly are. Clients long to be fully seen and heard from this deep, authentic space of Reality, recognizing and "joining" as the same essence, beyond all images.

Fully Present

When a coach really meets a client in the present moment, there is a sweet joining in the infinite, timeless, ground of being. Fully present is simply be-ing with another as the same source, and uniting beyond all stories of the past and/or projections of the future. Being fully present in the moment is total acceptance of what *is* right here, right now. Consciously being in the present is where nothing needs to change, nothing needs to be fixed, and nothing needs to be different. This is the recognition of life as it truly is. Deep listening comes from deep Presence; undistracted, fully engaged, interested, and not caught up in the thoughts passing through the mind. When fully present, there is quiet receptivity and awareness, making it possible to sense that which goes unsaid, but not unheard.

Radical Sincerity

Sincerely joining with another requires one to drop out of the personal me where thoughts, judgments, opinions, et cetera reside, and sink deep into the heart (Nirmala, 2008). Sinking deep into the heart-space, opening up, and feeling ones' expansiveness, gives way to genuine authenticity. When there is any sort of an agenda stemming from the coach; actions shift, and authentic connection is skewed. There is no longer a "clean" attentiveness; rather coaching filtered through passive intent, motivation, or desire. Entering into the world of the client and meeting him or her in his or her world of perception is one of the most kind, gentle, unimposing means to unite with someone's journey and really "be" with him or her with great authenticity and openness. Among other qualities, genuine authenticity is an experience of no façade, no roles or pretense, and no censoring.

Trusting Life

Is there anything we as coaches really know for sure about what our clients need? The second we think we know something, is the second we are in our heads with a feeling of disconnect from the ever-wise Life that naturally unfolds and shows precisely what is necessary. When a coach acts like he or she knows something that the client does not know about him or herself, it is disempowering, and teaches the client to lean on others and seek answers outside themselves. As clients begin to trust all communication coming from within, questions will naturally answer themselves and there will not be such a need to have the coach mirror back their own truth. This invites clients to trust their own internal process. The forever unknown gives a raw aliveness that meets what is needed in each and every moment.

A fundamental shift in identification and the elements that ensue are paramount to the growth and expansion of professional coaching. The timeless elements discussed above have tremendous impact on a coaching environment. They form the foundation for effective human interaction and authentic transformation. These unspoken elements exist while interacting with clients in a way that deeply touches and joins both coach and client from the very essence of the unseen and intangible. This unification cultivates an environment and interaction with depth and richness supportive for clear-seeing and grounded movement. This type of environment holds a container of space ripe for clarity and true freedom. This new coaching model will help bridge the gap between current coaching practice(s) and these unseen elements that arise from a fundamental shift in identification. I will further define these elements in detail in the upcoming chapters.

As mentioned above, this new coaching model, called, *Space to See Reality: A New Model for Professional Coaches,* is based on the research and literature relevant to this book. The model takes a close look at the elements as an engagement with form and from formlessness. It points to and discusses what this looks like in a manner that is applicable to any coaches' practice, regardless of the content or topic(s) of the specific coaching subject. The model will also outline the elements with great depth and detail, and include additional aspects (outlined below) to support coaches in their realistic application and implementation. Although these elements are beyond any skill-set, tool, belief, strategy, education, or technique, this book invites coaches to feel into these components, and engage with each one in a way that can really be felt, experienced, and shared with his or her clients. This new coaching model includes all aspects outlined in the first paragraph of this section, and will also include the following for each of the four elements:

- Its value to the coaching relationship
- Comprehensive and practical examples
- Exercises for coach clarity and experience
- Practical tools/suggestions for coaches for the clients' experience and understanding.

Unfortunately, not all, but many coaches lack the exposure, awareness, and/or practice with these elements. Many coaches not only lack this within themselves and their own lives, but also within their coach-client interactions. There is much in store for those coaches who find themselves interested to dive into the depths of this work. Those that are interested will begin to recognize and give greater attention to the subtle power and impact this shift in perspective has, and what benefits these elements contain. This new model is primarily for coaches interested in investigating a different approach to their coaching practice. It closes the gap in professional coaching, offering coaching clients the opportunity to discover their true selves, by engaging in various modes of active inquiry and silent stillness. Those coaches that have some experience with Consciousness, Awareness, Stillness, Mindfulness et cetera, might find this model easier to understand and utilize than those that do not have previous exposure to such studies. Considering there seems to be a void in a comprehensive model like this available, it's my hope that this work will be of great value and contribution in the field of professional coaching. Although this new model is intended specifically for professional coaches, it might also be quite useful for therapists, nurses, physicians, and anyone in the healing and helping professions who may be interested in taking a deeper look at the coach-client space.

1 EXPLORING "ME"
AND THE GROUND OF BEING

It's very, very important that we see and come to understand that this act of being identified with egoic consciousness is literally the root of all suffering. And so it's this root of all suffering that has to be really, closely examined and looked at. (Adyasanti, 2012b)

The idea that there is a "self"—separate and special and in charge of running "my" life—is purely an innocent mistake. It is simply a misunderstanding that there is some entity called "me" that exists. It is simply not true. As in, not true at all. This misunderstanding is the bedrock of all human suffering and turmoil. Suffering occurs in direct proportion to how much identity is derived from this illusive belief called "me." Through investigation, it appears that current coaching literature is founded on this false premise.

Most coaching literature appears similar to what Askew and Carenell sum up in *Transformative Coaching*;

With a stable sense of self-identity of a person: 1) in the conduct of day-to-day life will have created a defensive shell which "filters out" many of the dangers that threaten the integrity of the self, 2) is able to accept the integrity of the self as worthwhile, 3) will have a sufficient self-regard to sustain an active sense of the self – within the scope of reflexive control, rather than a passive sense of the self as an object in the world. (2011, p. 76)

Contrary to this, Professor of Cognitive Science and Epistemology, Francisco J. Varela (as cited in Senge et al., 2004) talks about the coming and going of the conceptual self, as "not a stable, solid entity . . . [the self is] constantly updating itself or renewing itself . . . So virtuality is not just an absence of a central self: it also has that kind of fragile flotation of coming and going" (p. 100). Basing one's concept of who I am on that which is a "fragile flotation of coming and going," can no wonder cause what Ken Wilber refers to as a "gnawing dissatisfaction of life" (1979, p. 85). You are that which does not come and go. As a coach, having a clear understanding of where this gnawing dissatisfaction of life stems from, can provide clarity to see the places clients get "stuck," and offer groundwork from which to move. All "stuck-ness" is the fruitless attempt to solve, change, or adjust this entity called "me" (that I take myself to be), which is in fact, not even real. Later we will discuss how seeing beyond this "fragile flotation" can offer opportunity for a tremendous shift (for lack of a better word) with clients.

Active Inquiry, Silent Stillness, and Practice:

1) *Have you ever noticed how the body changes, opinions changes, beliefs shift, career and interests come and go, and yet there is something here, a you, that feels the same year after year?*

In Elizabeth Topp's dissertation entitled, *Presence-Based Coaching:*

The Practice of Presence in Relation to Goal-Directed Activity, she reflects on a personal conversation she had with Adyashanti, a spiritual teacher who observes that, "we are always trying to create the perfect man. Transpersonal psychologists have brilliant minds, but the ideas are just another recycling of information" (2006, p. 30). This recycling of information and creating the "perfect man" or "me", is the effort to continue to develop, change, create, manipulate, heal, and mature the mind, the me; all of which has the capacity to continue the cycle of imprisonment of the mental world as the basis and premise of who we are. That being said, it appears quite evident that some people greatly benefit from time with a highly skilled therapist that works in the realm of the me, as there seems to be a time and place for such experiences in some individuals' evolution. Life coaching, as more specifically described in this model, provides opportunity to move beyond one's stories of me. It provides opportunity to begin to give recognition and deeper realization to this alternative mode of seeing and moving through the world; free from the suffering induced by the beliefs of who I am based on a fragile flotation.

This model is not another version of making a better me, thinking positively to be a stronger me, managing the me to a greater, more stable state, nor shuffling around beliefs, thoughts, and ideas to create an improved, more concrete version of this fragile flotation or me. This is not about painting the inside of our prison walls of "who I imagine my self to be" another color and adding decorative glitter. This is about seeing life free from this limited "me" identification as the basis of "who I am," and coaching from the Ground of Being; this open space that you truly are.

Active Inquiry, Silent Stillness, and Practice:

1) *What is looking from behind your eyes? What do you sense from the space behind your eyes? What is this space like right now? Is it open, expansive, and flowing freely? Or is it more limited and concentrated?*

2) *Just notice what is coming up right now. Notice if you are perceiving thoughts, sensations, et cetera from the mind. Notice what this is like. Now let your awareness drop down into your body, your heart-region, and notice what is seen, felt, and perceived from here. What is it like to see from here?*

3) *How do you experience other people when you feel/look from the heart-region?*

4) *Do thoughts have as big of a significance from this space?*

5) *To practice, pick a challenging situation with work/family et cetera. When you look at this situation from the heart-region, do you notice a spaciousness, an ease about it from here? Now try it from your mind. What do you notice? Do you feel constriction, friction, tension, and/or pointed-focus?*

Most people seek a coach when they hit a wall, are confronted with blockages, changes, uncertainties, confusion, or newness. When people say I want to be "free from suffering and struggle," "free from drama," "free from stress," "free from confusion," perhaps they are looking to be "free from" identification with the fragile flotation of held images, beliefs, and all subtle declarations of a confined, separate self as the foundation for who I am. This is, in and of itself, an inherent root of struggle, suffering, and internal conflict and war. Perhaps the yearning to be free from is contingent on the "freedom from" identification with thoughts, beliefs, and perceived identity as who I am. Living from something beyond the story of me is a very different perspective to explore and experience. Perhaps being free from, true freedom, rests in the very recognition of life as you really are; free from the identification as a perceived separate self. If you want to experience freedom, consider this concept of "me" may not be real.

Struggle and dissatisfaction are symbols of identification with this perceived fragile flotation, also known as the self or me. Wilber (1979) speaks about dissatisfaction and suffering as the graceful springboard for seeing life from a different space, a truer reality:

> The movement of descent and discovery begins the moment you consciously become dissatisfied with life. Contrary to most professional opinion, this gnawing dissatisfaction with life is not a sign of 'mental illness', nor an indication of poor social adjustment, or a character disorder. For concealed within this basic unhappiness with life and existence is the embryo of a growing intelligence, a special intelligence usually buried under the immense weight of social shams. A person who is beginning to sense the suffering of life is, at the same time, beginning to awaken to deeper realities, truer realities. For suffering smashes to pieces the complacency of our normal fictions about reality, and forces us to become alive in a special sense—to see carefully, to feel deeply, to touch ourselves and our worlds in ways we have heretofore avoided. It has been said, and I truly think, that all suffering is the first grace. In a special sense, suffering is almost a time of rejoicing, for it marks the birth of creative insight. (p. 85)

The beautiful thing about dissatisfaction and suffering is that it is a clear indication—a red flag—a felt visceral sense of living from misidentification. Suffering is a knock at the door, a wake-up call bringing attention to that which might not be completely true. It's the very doorway to realizing something more real, bringing inherent freedom from the perceived confinement of old conditioning.

Active Inquiry, Silent Stillness, and Practice:

1) *In what ways do you feel a gnawing dissatisfaction of life?*

2) *What is your experience of how suffering shows up, smashing to pieces your beliefs about reality?*

3) *If dissatisfaction and suffering are signs of belief(s) in a separate self, how might you respond to these gnawing sensations when they arise?*

4) *How might you respond and work with your clients to do the same?*

Recognition beyond the personal me - seeing through the gnawing dissatisfaction of life - asks one to take an honest look at the images that are believed to be true about who I am. Take a close look; inquire into the definitions you have bought into about you/life that do not actually hold validity. Through the belief of these definitions often comes confusion, suffering, and a "stuckness." When we believe in those ideas which run in opposition to how things actually are, we suffer the consequences through experiencing confusion, frustration, doubt, et cetera. Suffering is experienced in direct proportion to the degree of exclusive identification with this illusive, non-existent, self. Fear, and all its relatives, is one sign that we have identified as something (an image of me) that is simply not congruent with reality; with what actually is. Identification with an image (any image that is claimed to be me) is simply another smoke-screen layer built up over our true Self. This can create clogs in the porousness of what is really here; the suchness of nothingness that we are. These smoke-screen layers exclusively identifying with something that is not true is actually the foundation for inner conflict and suffering, and yet are the doorway to seeing Life as it really is.

Active Inquiry, Silent Stillness, and Practice:

Judgment, ideas, beliefs, dreams, desires, fears, worries, opinions, and concepts are the many ways we limit our experience of reality, and thereby limit our experience of our true nature. These concepts do not limit true nature, but limit our experience of it.

1) *Choose an opinion that you really believe to be true. Notice the sense you have of yourself as you do this. Does holding this create openness and expansiveness?*

2) *Do you feel more connected with others and the world, or do you feel more separate and apart from the world?*

3) *Is the narrative you are believing to be true, really, fully true?*

4) *How might you identify these blockages your clients stumble on?*

Recognition beyond the personal me is more of an un-learning than a learning process. It challenges what one is identified as, which is often the very foundation for who you take yourself to be. This is the very "fire of grace," the dismantling of false concepts that were the ground in which you thought you stood upon and used to hold so true. This unlearning is a type of deconstruction rather than self-constructing enhancement process. Unlearning brings a sense of clarity to life as it really is, with a sense of transparent freedom. As you begin to see through these faulty, quicksand beliefs as the basis and truth of who you are, there is an opening to that which is deeper, truer. As our concepts of self disintegrate, or as Wilber says, are "smashed to pieces," by the fire of Love, we are left in new territory to see and touch the very essence of Life as it actually is. Although this is often a disorienting experience, it is truly a kind of fire of grace, bringing one back to reality.

Questioning ones' beliefs is a powerful way to begin to see the futility of the beliefs and concepts causing suffering. Peeling away thoughts and images that we take to be real, and living from/as Vast Transparency, is really the crux to getting unstuck and experiencing authentic liberation. This premise is paramount to any mindfulness-type coaching practice, and yet is a foundation which has yet to be deeply explored in this growing profession:

> At the root of my depression was the sense that I was a separate person—an individual me, an entity separate from life itself and divided from the moment. . . . Although we may not all be clinically depressed, we all walk around with stories about ourselves; we all are trying to make our lives go the way we want them to. And we are all failing on some level to be who we are not. (Foster, 2012, p. 22)

What would it be like to be free from this separate "I" that is nothing but all the made-up images, beliefs, opinions, et cetera that are taken to be who you are?

As Albert Einstein says, "Once you can accept the universe as matter expanding into nothing that is something, wearing stripes with plaid comes easy"(2013). The more this expansive you is recognized as the Essence of who you are, illusory blinders fall away or burn up in a way that allows for a space of transparency, openness, and a richness of vibrant liberation. This unleashes clarity, exposing whatever is hidden and ready to be seen that is possibly causing friction, confusion, stuck-ness, and suffering.

Active Inquiry, Silent Stillness, and Practice:

1) *What if you saw life from an open and porous, broad and deep, expansive and limitless space, void of division and finite concepts of time, with the recognition and rich texture of vast freedom?*

2) *What if the real you were actually comprised of and encompassed much more than the perceived boundaries and limitations of this emotional and physical body?*

3) *If it were true that who you really are encompassed something much larger than the confines of the physical, mental, and emotional 'body,' how might that change your coaching relationship(s)?*

4) *Take a moment and just close your eyes. How might coaching look from beyond all thought, belief, opinion, and judgment, and from this unlimited, transparent space?*

5) *What profound impact might this have in a coaching relationship when moving from this space?*

Active Inquire and Silent Stillness are two primary ways to begin to peel away the many false beliefs, images, and ideas of "who I think I am," and to begin to see and experience true essence. It is vital that thinking is questioned. Active inquiry is a way to question any thought or belief to see if it has any validity. The desire to really see one's own illusions is the key to getting clear and unstuck. Byron Katie, spiritual teacher and founder of a questioning process called The Work, shares:

> I discovered that when I believed my thoughts, I suffered, but that when I didn't believe them, I didn't suffer, and that this is true for every human being. Freedom is as simple as that. I found that suffering is optional. I found a joy within me that has never disappeared, not for a single moment. That joy is in everyone, always. (Katie, 2013)

Katie describes The Work as:

> A simple yet powerful process of inquiry that teaches you to identify and question the thoughts that cause all the suffering in the world. It's a way to understand what's hurting you, and to

address the cause of your problems with clarity. (Katie, 2013)

Katie's Work offers a way to question thinking. There are many ways in which to do this. Choosing a belief that triggers fear, worry, judgment, et cetera is a great place to start. For example, if I'm worried that "I won't know enough for my client," and I believe the thought, "As the coach, I should know all the answers to my clients' questions," I will likely feel fear and anxiety when believing this to be true. Fear and anxiety are often prime indicators of believing in something not fully true. Simply questioning this thought can bring clarity and freedom. Asking, "Is it true?" opens the possibility of seeing the unreality of believed thoughts. This creates space between the believed thought and reality.

Silent Stillness is the other primary way to become aware of the conditioned thought patterns that skew one's perception of true Being. Gangaji, spiritual author and teacher, often says, "Just STOP . . . this moment, stop, right where you are" (Gangaji, 2009). Sitting still provides space to see the loops of cyclical thinking that keep one stuck in patterns of mental clutter. Sitting still often slows the mental jargon. When busyness slows down, patterned thinking (that is at the root) is exposed. Sitting still offers opportunity to notice the peace and stillness beneath the swirls of thought, and provides opportunity to notice the ways thought still has a magnetic grip on ones' experience. Sitting with that which arises can often bring fear. As Adyashanti shares, "When people sit down and meditate it's not at all uncommon for fear to arise at some point" (2006, p. 31). Many people avoid sitting still for this very reason. They don't want to sit still with the nagging, uncomfortable thoughts that they take to be real. Sitting still also offers quiet space to just Be. Sitting still, and simply letting everything be as it actually is, gives space to notice all the clever ways there is avoidance, or resistance, to what is. Various methods of Sitting Still (or some call this Meditation) are offered throughout the next several chapters.

2 DENSITY AND TRANSPARENCY WITH CLIENTS

The ultimate state is to become so transparent that everything that arises internally and everything that happens externally is met without any resistance or any holding on. Everything is allowed to be just the way it is without any judgment or effort to change it or hang on to it. Nothing is taken personally. Everything just flows easily from and through your being with nothing in the way, as if you were transparent. This quality of transparency is why we enjoy being around spiritual teachers. Whatever you say to them neither offends nor flatters them. Nothing sticks. Everything just passes through them freely. The same is true for whatever comes out of them: there is no blocking, censoring, or strategizing. It's a beautiful thing to be around this kind of transparency (Nirmala, 2007, p. 53).

So long as you are identifying as this separate I, with beliefs, attachments, and conclusions about who you are, there will be dense areas within you that clients can encounter, consciously or unconsciously. Transparency is a term that is often used to describe being open and on the table with whatever is on one's mind and in one's thoughts, emotions, and feelings. This is not the transparency that I am speaking about here. I am speaking about an open field, this Vast Space void of identification with the illusory concepts of me, where the coach and client actually, truly meet, and where present aliveness and deep vitality can be touched and experienced.

Varela (as cited in Senge et al., 2004) touches on the effect on clients of how you show up:

> You know, the paradox of being more real means to be much more virtual and therefore less substantial and less determined . . . A life of wisdom consists of being constantly engaged in that letting go, and letting the virtuality of the fragility of the self manifest itself. When you are with somebody who really has that capacity to a full-blown level, it affects you. When you meet those kinds of people, you enter into a kind of resonance with them. You relax—there's something very enjoyable about that way of being. There's a joy in that kind of life. (p. 100–101)

There is an immense spaciousness in the presence of someone that is free of identification with the "fragile" self; the "fragile" conglomeration of impulses, images, conditioning, and beliefs we so often take ourselves to be, that hold no reality.

Active Inquiry, Silent Stillness, and Practice:

1) *What is it like to give space to an experience?*
2) *What is it like to give space to the full spectrum of emotions, thoughts, and feelings that arise within you, without identifying as them?*
3) *How freeing is it to be in the presence of someone that is not needing to change, fix, defend, or push away that which is here? How do you experience these people? What do you notice?*
4) *What effect does it have on you?*

5) *When giving someone space to fully and authentically show up, do you notice the ability to perceive more of his or her true Essence?*

6) *How much open space—free of sticky, dense belief structures—is offered in your client sessions?*

In *Living from the Heart*, Nirmala states:

What you really are is pure awareness—empty space that has this miraculous ability to sense the world . . . Awareness is a quality of space itself and not contained in your head, chest, or belly. What actually senses is this infinite space that is all around the physical body. (2008, p. 37)

We all have the capacity to intuitively feel, consciously or unconsciously, the openness and transparency of those around, or conversely the blocks that can have people feel walled off, distant, and unapproachable. These stuck areas of believed images and thoughts are what your clients can feel (or bump into). The more in tune you are with the spaciousness that you are, the more in tune you will be with the spaciousness of your clients. And, the more in tune you are with the dynamic of lived out conditioning and beliefs with yourself (where you are stuck in believed thought/image), the more in tune you will be to seeing these stuck places in your clients and have a greater ability to work with him or her in this capacity.

Beliefs and held meaning that do not align with reality can create limitations in the coach/client relationship; containing, smothering, and possibly inhibiting full, widespread potential. Who you take yourself to be, that seemingly endless list of images and beliefs, are the very walls that your clients can consciously or unconsciously bump up against. Illusory false concepts can feel like dense walls. These walls are nothing more than the concepts of the believed me. When clients bump up against these dense beliefs, it can feel

41

constricting, containing, and as though there is lack of air to breathe and freedom to openly speak. These barriers of "me" can make it significantly more challenging for clients to feel a sense of freedom to open up, reveal vulnerability, share with authenticity, and expose his or her own illusions and challenges; all of which are the doorway to liberation. When a client's image of "me" differs from his or her coaches' image of "me," it can cause friction, contraction, or a lack of desire to open. Offering an unobtrusive environment for clients to explore deep within themselves is valuable beyond measure. When residing in your mind—giving focused attention to the thoughts in your head—there is a solid density (of internal commentary, ideas, beliefs, etc.) that exists regardless of verbal exchange. This solid density creates constriction, and potentially inhibits the clients' ability to be completely vulnerable and exposed; the very space where authentic change often takes place. When we are consumed with thoughts and judgments, we are not able to experience full connection with clients. These opinions and beliefs keep us at a distance from what is actually present, and gets in the way of fully connecting with our clients. True meeting can only take place in the absence of the walls of my "self." Who is having conversation?

Active Inquiry, Silent Stillness, and Practice:

1) *Have you ever been in the presence of someone that you feel you can tell anything to and it would all somehow be okay to share?*

2) *Conversely, have you ever been around someone that no matter what you say, they have something to negate, combat, agree with, or disagree about?*

3) *When in conversation with someone, have you ever felt certain topics were off limits? ...like you're bumping into certain beliefs, concepts, or opinions that limited your desire or ability to openly share and explore?*

4) *What's it like to be around someone like this?*

5) *What concepts do you believe to be true, that might not actually be real, that clients may bump into and limit potential?*

When the coach's perceptual world is melted away through the recognition and attention of life beyond thought, there is an opening—an infinite spaciousness—that is porous and free. This infinite spaciousness is free of judgment, free of limitation, free of certainties, and free of the dense personal me that obstructs spacious Being. It is free of the personal me that is filled with innumerable words of advice, direction, and ideas, filtered through layers of personal perception and belief. This me offers an array of strategies, plans, and ways in which to change, fix, get rid of, gather, and/or manipulate that which is actually present and happening. This is just what the mind does; it compares, judges, coerces, and tries to fix. The mind is constant commentary, creating stories about what is truly here right now. This constant commentary is, as Eckhart Tolle says in *The Power of Now*, "unnecessary judgment, resistance to what *is*, and denial of the Now" (1999, p. 76). The porousness of life as it really is, is void of the dense illusion of the conceptual, separate me.

Active Inquiry, Silent Stillness, and Practice:

Don't judge what you see. Don't make it wrong, or bad. Simply be curious, inquire, and listen.

1) *Without judging what shows up, ask yourself, how porous am I? How clear am I of these layers of thoughts and beliefs that I take to be true and real?*

2) *What are my "triggers" and "hot buttons" of beliefs and definitions that set me into thinking, resisting, evaluating, and super-imposing with clients, consciously or unconsciously?*

3) *The truth is freedom. In what ways am I putting myself to "sleep" and limiting my experience of freedom?*

Take a minute and think about a client, that when in their presence, you experience tension and constriction in your body. When asking these questions, see what arises and jot down on paper what layers you notice coming up.

4) *Ask yourself, what is it that is being said that I might not want to be hearing or experiencing?*

5) *What ways might I be prematurely jumping in to try to "save" my client from experiencing what he or she is experiencing? What ways might I be cutting him or her off, diverting topics, or jumping in because I am perhaps uncomfortable with their discomfort? And again, what is it that is being said that you might not want to be hearing or experiencing?*

These layers of believed thoughts and certainties can be felt like a brick wall; solid, dense, separate, blocking out, and limiting. When clients bump into these unresolved layers of "me" in a coach, it has a strong potential to create an environment felt to be restrictive and less conducive and available for broad openings. A transparent, open, and spacious offering provides fertile ground for clients to feel safe and welcomed, offering spaciousness where everything is already allowed and accepted, open and free to take risks, room to deeply inquire, expose vulnerability, and share raw authenticity. This transparent space is where emotions and sensations are allowed to arise and be seen exactly as they are, and where one's perspective has unlimited space to be lovingly welcomed and investigated.

Active Inquiry, Silent Stillness, and Practice:

1) *What thoughts and beliefs do you notice that arise during coaching sessions?*

2) *How close and connected can/do you feel with your client from this place of thinking?*

3) *How might connecting from the mind impact your sessions with clients?*

Now drop into the fullness of your Being.

4) *What do you notice about the connectedness from here?*

5) *How might things change in your client sessions if you were to connect from this space?*

This infinite, open field is where learned beliefs, opinions, conditioned concepts, and shoulds simply do not exist, and resistance to what is actually occurring is null and void. It is here, in this space that there is an opening, a spacious clearing without the hooks of the thinking mind that snag one back into seeing and living from the limited, illusive, personal self. It is here where there is an invitation to feel at home, to feel free, and to walk into and move from one's true nature. It is here where all needs are met, all questions actually disintegrate, all necessary direction is heard, and where raw brilliance is revealed. This is where the form and the formless dance, coexisting as one. Form seems to disappear and the reality of who we are opens into a spacious freedom to life exactly as it is; transparent, lucid, porous, and free of the dense form of the identification with the separate me, free of the illusion that the thinking mind and all the grand thoughts floating through have deep significance or real importance. Transparency is one of the ultimate invitations for freedom, providing opportunity to really see oneself through the veil of illusion, beyond the image of who we take ourselves to be, free from and beyond the mask and very barriers that bring suffering.

Wade (1996) talks about development and Becoming as descriptions for moving in stages from identification with self, to liberation from this identification. He describes development as an individual that has gained the capacity to self-reflect and be conscious of what was previously, routinely unconscious. He terms Becoming as the individual that still considers him or herself existentially separate and this "separation in time is part of a dualistic sequence, where this moment is still being succeeded by another one, so that the individual's orientation is always one of becoming rather than being rooted in the Eternal Now" (p. 204). Although this is not another personal development model, this does honor personal development programs, as becoming aware of the "stages" clients may experience is crucial to coaching from this space.

Active Inquiry, Silent Stillness, and Practice:

A coach's awareness of his or her own mental/psychological terrain is paramount.

1) *Do you offer an open space for clients to freely walk into?*

2) *How can you listen, move, and speak from this space free from the identification of me?*

3) *What does it "look" like to really listen from this deep Stillness beyond all the concepts?*

4) *What does it mean to listen, speak, and see from the head versus the open spaciousness of the heart and the totality of your being?*

5) *What beliefs do you hold tightly that create dense walls, inhibiting fully open connectivity with your clients?*

6) *Are there thoughts that have strength, stickiness, meaning, or importance?*

7) *What are the belief structures and blockages within you that can potentially be sensed by your clients, and possibly create the desire to defend against or avoid raising certain topics?*

8) *What do you identify as, that clients may intuitively perceive?*

Part II

PERMEATING ELEMENTS

PRESENTING PERMEATING ELEMENTS

It is essential to begin to fill the gap between the premise of current coaching literature, and the foundation derived from ancient and contemporary literature. Shifting into this latter alternative premise also presents elements not yet explored in professional coaching. Within this work, I suggest and describe a paradigm shift from current professional coaching approaches, to an alternative premise rooted in ancient and contemporary studies. Currently, the premise for coaching literature is based on personal identification with ideas, beliefs, and thoughts as the basis of who I am. However, the alternative perspective points to, and is based upon, the fundamental shift of one's identification from the thoughts, ideas, and stories of conditioned thinking as the basis of who I am, to one's identity as a timeless, unchanging and formless Essence. When this spaciousness is recognized as the very ground of one's true being, the elements contained here-in are a natural outcome in how you show up. Herein is an exploration of the intangible elements that arise from this shift in perspective within the coaching environment.

3 JOINING OR RECOGNIZING SAMENESS-ONENESS

We are all walking around presenting an image to each other, and we're relating to each other as images. Whoever we think somebody else is, it's just an image we have in our mind. When we relate to each other from the standpoint of image, we're not relating to who each other is, we're just relating to our imagination of who each other is. Then we wonder why we don't relate so well, why we get into arguments, and why we misunderstand each other so deeply. (Adyashanti, 2011, p. 20)

I am who you are. There is nothing but the One in relationship with itself.

When you have dropped out of your head (out of the thinking mind) and into that more expansive, all-inclusive space (often felt as the heart-space), you are in a place where joining with another can truly take place. Images melt away, smoke screens of beliefs simply vanish, and there is an authentic meeting void of walls and barriers of thought, opinion, and judgment. There is a quiet, deep connection; a oneness in joining from Essence, this Ground of Being. There is a sense of rest and stillness, rooted in the substance of Vast Space, rather than disconnect of separation, barriers of thought and division. It is here that the playing field, so to speak, is even. There is no hierarchy, no pecking order, no positions, and no authority of any sort. The thinking mind that generates thoughts and beliefs of differences, comparisons, and opinions of better than, worse than, or different from, is in the back seat.

Believed thoughts by their very nature create division and separation. Giving attention to thoughts of division can take hold and keep you from connecting with your clients from a clear place of oneness. When we entertain and believe thoughts of separation and division, comparison and hierarchy, we suffer, and so does our connection with those sitting with us. In this dream of division we miss each other. The word joining is even a bit untrue to use here, as it inherently suggests a separate you and a me coming together from separation. Recognizing is a more accurate description, as it is just a witnessing of the oneness that already is. Without the thought of you and me, there is nothing but openness, sameness—a sweet recognition (feeling of joining) of wholeness. This sameness is the oneness of Life. As Nirmala says in his book, *Nothing Personal*:

> The concepts about who we are create artificial boundaries between ourselves and the rest of the world. These boundaries aren't solid or real but permeable, like the border between two states. All of our concepts are like that; they create unreal boundaries. (2007, p. 58)

Active Inquiry, Silent Stillness, and Practice:

1)   How do you entertain and experience unreal boundaries of differences in your interactions with clients?

2) Are you aware of the patterns of thinking that create division and separation between you and your clients?

Try holding on to a belief about your client. Notice the sensations that flow through when you really believe this thought.

3) Does the thought bring contraction, or bring relaxation and connection?

If you really believe this thought, then the sense of this me will contract as long as the idea is held. You will experience a contraction in correlation to the truth of the belief held. When sensing openness, softening, and expansion, these are clues you are experiencing more of the truth of your being. When you notice the mind wandering off, simply bring attention back to the breath, and ground in what is here. You can do this same thing with your clients.

As Nirmala sums up:

> The "me", the sense of your self, is no longer felt to be so limited or small. It becomes more complete and unbounded. The boundaries soften and dissolve, and any sense of inadequacy, limitation, or deficiency is lessened or eliminated. (2007, p. 88)

What Do You See?

In Jeff Foster's book, *The Deepest Acceptance*, he shares, "Perhaps that's what life needs more than anything—people who no longer see problems, but who see the inseparability of themselves and the world and who fully engage with the world from that place" (2012, p. 28). What do you see when you look at your client(s)? Where do you see him or her from? Where you see your client from is probably one of the most important components in a coaching relationship. Foster continues:

> In seeing how perfect somebody is, exactly as they are, you are freer than ever to help them take a look at what they perceive as imperfection. You're no longer coming from the root assumption that they are a broken thing that needs fixing. (p. 28)

Where you see from, and how you see your clients, "sets the stage" to a spacious openness, ripe and inviting to look at that which is unconscious.

For example, most clients probably show up at your office identified as _____ (fill in the blank); Essence appearing as _____ persona. This could be anything—man, woman, successful, unsuccessful, smart, dumb, depressed, mom, brother, rich, poor, victim, the one that suffers, et cetera. The list of identification can and often does appear endless. As a coach, you have the choice in how you meet clients; how you see your clients. Regardless of the kind of coaching you do, the way in which you see your clients—the place from where you see them—can absolutely have a tremendous impact on your interactions.

When you really look at a client from vast transparency, or the Ground of Being, there is opportunity to recognize true Essence. Rather than seeing clients as the persona presented, you can begin to see true Being simply appearing with a current story. When looking at a client through the lens of the thinking mind, there are usually endless thoughts passing through. When thoughts are believed, perspective shifts and Reality appears clouded or severely restricted. Seeing is then from a very limited, narrow perspective. What exists beyond what we can currently see or perceive to be here is still present, your perception simply shrinks and awareness of total reality just appears smaller and smaller. A horse with blinders can only see that which is directly in front of him or her; nothing more. Thoughts can act like blinders; only allowing you to see a small percentage of the total, actual picture. Some stories and experiences come and go; fluctuating, contradicting, and changing by the second. Other stories and experiences linger and appear to have more of an imprint and cyclical hold. Most humans move through life based on lingering recycled loops of patterned thinking. These blinding infinite ideas, thoughts, conclusions, and opinions can run amuck when residing solely in your head. Thoughts themselves are not the issue. Believing thoughts as total Reality is what causes clouded vision, a feeling of disconnect, and the struggle or inability to recognize Essence. Coaching from the mind is often where we see clients as the persona they are presenting themselves to be, rather than seeing them as the Vastness they truly are.

Active Inquiry, Silent Stillness, and Practice:

1) *What ways does your awareness of that which is all around, become limited?*

2) *What are the blinders of belief that cloud your perspective of Reality?*

3) *Do you see clients as this misperception, misidentification of a person with problems?*

4) *Do you see him or her as a person with an issue to solve? Or do you see him or her as Being with a believed story that is causing internal conflict and confusion?*

5) *Is it possible to really see a client as true Being while simultaneously embracing the believed story they bring to the coaching session?*

6) *How might you see from this open space of Reality, without denying the story he or she is bringing to the surface? What might this look like?*

To be seen as Essence, known as Essence, and humanly

embraced amidst the appearing persona is a beautiful gift. As Lasley et al. state, "Transformation happens when people are deeply seen, heard, understood, and recognized for their gifts" (2011, p. 6). I would even say that when people are deeply seen, heard, understood, and recognized as the very Essence of who they truly are—while embracing the human experience—transformation happens. Humans long to be truly seen and heard from this deep, authentic space of Reality. There is a yearning to be seen beyond the images presented, beyond the barriers believed to protect, and beyond all conditioning. Humans yearn to be seen for his or her true Self, to be fully authentic, and to feel acceptance. To be seen and recognized from Being to Being, offers an opening to feel connected to wholeness, to fall back into Home.

Life Meeting Itself

As we have covered earlier, most coaching models, handbooks, manuals, literature, and courses teach strategy and skill from the perspective of a you and a me; the very foundation of separation and division. One of the biggest gifts any coach can offer is unspoken, meeting in the dimension beyond words and thought. Recognizing Being-ness, that vibrant-aliveness in-as everything and everyone is connective beyond words and without effort. This unspoken gift of recognition is the heart of truly meeting with another, and more accurately stated, truly meeting oneself as another. It is the same space, the same life, the same Being-ness seen in "the other." Really, it is simply Life recognizing itself in another, as itself. There is no longer separation, no longer a me and a you. There is simply a continuum, connecting as, not connecting to. This is Love;

connected as Source felt within you. It is Life relating; Life meeting Life in form, appearing as another. This is where true joining, true relating, true connecting happens; in the recognition of non-separation, oneness. There is nothing but the One in relationship with itself. This is one of the biggest gifts any coach offers; the recognition of that Being-ness as everyone and everything, in another, as another.

Prajna Ana's book, *Dying Into This*, is described by unidentified sellers as, "This book supports and cultivates the goodness of each individual by reminding them of their true heart, thereby restoring a deep connection to all of life. Only once we each get in touch with that can any real, positive change happen" (Amazon, 2013) Ana elaborates saying, "It is undeniable how connected we all are – to God, to self, and to each other. Once this is seen, we move from love – and that is how we will transform the world – one heart at a time" (Amazon, 2013) True meeting is beyond the surface of the human "dream" in the deep Be-ingness of Life.

Coming Home to this wholeness is to realize your own completion, and to wake up from the dream of separation. Separation, a belief in the me as who I am, is the very root of suffering. Suffering often drives one to seek wholeness; sometimes through the guise of seeking happiness, fulfillment, completion, worthiness, et cetera. Wholeness, oneness, is what the heart really seeks in oneself and in another. There is a deep yearning to join in this capacity, to see and recognize wholeness, true essence.

Active Inquiry, Silent Stillness, and Practice:

1) *What might happen from this place of no other in a coach/client relationship?*

2) *How might this sameness-oneness be experienced by a client?*

3) *What might the client notice when joining with you from this same, connected space?*

4) *How might the possibilities be different when meeting from this connected, unified space?*

Meeting in this unshakable Presence ends the search for love, joy, freedom, security, and the need for things to be other than what they are in this very moment. If our natural state of being is this vast open space of wholeness and completeness, when there is a feeling of separation there is a natural yearning to reconnect, to join in this oneness, this sameness that is the actuality of life. Humans suffer when (in the head) believing thoughts of differences, division, and separation. When in the heart of Essence, there is an alive-Presence that can be experienced; an intimacy closer than ones' own breath. All humans long to feel connected, undivided, and whole; it is our natural state of being. The longing to feel connected to oneself, to Life itself, can be traced back to one of humanity's core sources of suffering.

Seeing a client from Presence, as Presence, invites the client to tap into this vastness for themselves. As Nelson Mandela says, "as we let our own light shine, we unconsciously give other people permission to do the same" (Williamson, 2008). As a coach, offering space to meet in Presence is liberating. There is nothing to hide, nothing to cover up, nothing to be afraid of, and nothing to change. This invitation to drop all facades, all self-proclaimed images, all streams of mental chatter, and all perceptions of who we think we are is truly a beautiful offering. Coaching from this space invites clients to experience their own freedom beyond the limited self, as they feel into and experience this liberation with you. In this sweet joining, the recognition in oneself and in another allows room for new insights and clarity in the Reality of who we really are. True wisdom is born from Presence, and ignites clarity, authenticity, and vitality. In *Hidden Treasure*, Gangaji shares that:

> It is part of our nature as humans to wonder and to imagine our life freed of its relative constraints. When we meet someone who has—or even only appears to have—a promise of liveliness unknown to us, we are liable to catch a spark of it. That spark can spell destruction or disruption to our harmonious, protective cocoon. (2011, p. 81)

When clients see Life in you, it simply mirrors back, reminding them of that same Life as them. Existential psychologist, Heine Kohut said what human beings need most is the mirroring presence of others (as cited in Bryson 2004, p. 101). This mirroring can be quite liberating, and can also cause one to feel temporarily unstable as they no longer lean on images of illusion that were formerly ones' foundation. Underneath the unstable images is the substance of vastness and freedom that can ultimately be seen and experienced.

Active Inquiry, Silent Stillness, and Practice:

1) *As you move from Essence, from this free flowing spaciousness, do you notice your ability to respond to what is actually taking place rather than just reacting to the words that are spoken or persona presented?*

2) *When seeing from this space, do you notice a shift in your clients' ability to drop out of identification with this dream world and meet you in this quiet space?*

3) *Do you notice clients avoiding meeting you here?*

4) *Do you notice a discomfort with your client when you really see him or her from this spaciousness?*

5) *Do you notice a comfort with your client when you really see him or her from this space?*

6) *What fears come up for you when you meet a client from here?*

7) *How might this "meeting" change your interactions?*

8) *How might this "meeting" change how they show up?*

When connecting from vast Awereness and not the mind, there is no longer the coach, the teacher, the client, or the other. There is obviously a "facilitator" of the session, but there is a sameness, a oneness where the "other" does not really exist. Being sees Being, beyond form. Being is aware of and is attending to Being, without thought. When connecting—seeing from this place—this oneness of all humanity becomes clear. There is no other "out" there. There is only us, this. As Jeff Foster shares, "In the absence of a separate person, you discover all of humanity" (2012, p. 91). How beautiful that we can truly meet without words, beyond education and skills, and without our knowingness and certainties. Enter this still Presence and watch these passing thoughts of differences vanish into the nothingness from which they arrived. How liberating! No filters, no smoke screens; simply raw life. What a beautiful invitation to taste authentic wholeness and true "connectivity."

Flow

This "uniting" is a fluidity; a sense of flow that naturally springs forth. Within the "flow" there is no efforting (no "effort-er"), no struggle, no force, no "doer." This is our natural state. In Flow there is no "I," no illusory "person" clogging the fluidity. Life is simply operating and moving, free of the glitches of the me, and free of separation and division. Nothing but fear, judgment, opinion, worry, manipulation, et cetera can inhibit or block this natural flow. Resting in this natural state of ease releases the flow of uninhibited Life. This natural state has the capacity to evoke this flow with others. Attentive awareness in the present now is where there is possibility to experience the "capacity for flow and insight" (Seligman, 2002, p. 5).

Csikszentmihalyi wrote a book called, *Beyond Boredom and Anxiety* (2000) where they recorded research and experiments on various subjects regarding the state of Flow. In this state of "effortless absorption," there is a loss of reflective self-consciousness (p. 91), and regardless of the activity of the interviewee, the experience was noted to be "rewarding in and of itself." When one is not "self"-focused or "self"-conscious—absorbed in the minds' activity—one may notice this effortless flow with clients, naturally attending to the present moment.

Topp (as cited in Csikszentmihalyi & Larson, 1978) presents the idea that there are positive and negative aspects that result from Flow:

> Unique to the Flow state is the "selective or limited" attention that one gives to the activity without awareness of self, others or the environment. Thus while the Flow state is often associated with optimal performance, potential negative consequences exist due to the loss of larger field of awareness that may include both one's own needs as well as the needs of others. (p. 66)

For this reason, Topp breaks up Flow into parts, including "mindfulness," which she defines as "an intentional practice in which the actor consciously opens one's attention to include the broad field of awareness and all its contents"[p. 66]. Topp points to the idea that, "Flow narrows and focuses attention, while mindfulness broadens and opens one's attentional field" (p. 67).

Thich Nhat Hahn (1995) describes mindfulness as "what is going on within and all around us" (p. 14). It is in this author's perspective that Flow, in what Thich Nhat Hahn describes as mindfulness, is inclusive of all internal and external—focused as well as broadly aware—shifting forward and back within both, of which is not necessarily negative or positive, but simply movement in and out from moment to moment. This full spectrum leaves one open and receptive to the natural shifting of focused engagement, and a broad awareness of the greater field of the external environment.

Active Inquiry, Silent Stillness, and Practice:

1) *What might it be like to offer this "united-sameness" environment with your clients?*

2) *What might it look like, feel like?*

3) *If the recognition of connectivity and sameness were the only thing that shifted within you, what might be the possibilities within a coaching session?*

The yearning to feel connected is probably one of the most sought after feelings and experiences with all humans. Feeling disconnected from Life itself can be extremely painful, confusing, heart wrenching, and disorienting.

4) *What if you offered an environment conducive for clients to feel their wholeness, their own connection to Life simply through joining with them from this space?*

5) *Is it possible that clients simply see a mirror of themselves while sitting with their coach?*

6) *If this is so, how are you showing up in each of your sessions?*

Joining or Recognizing in Oneness-Sameness is the end of a

separate entity, the end of me separate from you, and the end of the me separate from Source. "It is undeniable how connected we all are – to God, to self, and to each other. Once this is seen, we move from love – and that is how we will transform the world – one heart at a time" (Ana, 2013).

4 FULLY PRESENT

"There's nowhere for you to get to—you're just here" (Neill, 2011).

We are surrounded by subtle and not so subtle ploys suggesting ways to make a better, happier, stronger, more satisfied, and complete "me." These strong suggestions are everywhere. Society offers innumerable ways in which to turn from our unconditioned awareness, denying its very existence. It seems quite unfortunate that society appears to be set up for a denial of Being with all the ploys to get sucked into serving my "self." Completeness is advertised as something that is anywhere other than already here. This collective belief is everywhere you turn. And yet these empty promises of fulfillment and completeness other than being already here, is the very gnawing sensation calling us "home" to our open awareness, where unshakable fulfillment exists.

There is an overarching, collective belief system that things need to be different than the way they actually are. This is the continual distraction away from what is, into commentary of what should or should not be, ought to be or not, and needs to be or cannot. Coming home to the present, total acceptance of this right here, where nothing needs to change, nothing needs to be fixed, and nothing needs to be different, is the recognition of life as it truly is. This Presence is the end of conditioned, cyclical thinking and suffering. Not wanting to fully be oneself as is—resisting the complete spectrum of aspects of yourself or of what is actually here—creates suffering. This is disempowering. It takes you out of yourself, out of the here and now. Coaching from that which is all already accepted supports liberation. Acceptance is a "yes" to all that already is, and supports client movement beyond perceived limitations and barriers.

Active Inquiry, Silent Stillness, and Practice:

Theorist John Welwood (2000) describes what he calls Pure Presence, as a stance of resting in open presence within whatever arises, which is no other than 'pure being'" (p. 97).

1) *So what would it be like in this space where nothing is a problem, nothing needs to change to experience freedom and happiness?*

2) *What would it be like in this space where everything that arises is simply a part of the beauty, naturalness, depth and fullness of life itself?*

3) *What if you could experience life from an open and spacious perspective where there is room for everything?*

4) *What if you could experience life where there is room for all of what is really appearing?*

5) *What if you could experience life without the need to block out, deny, or resist anything that shows up?*

The depth of your Being can hold it all. "Standing authentically in a question; we are open to the situation and present to its possibilities" (Hyde, 1995, p. 14). Showing up, fully present, is an indescribable offering. It is one of the fundamental elements in establishing authentic space for openness, vulnerability, innocence, and a safe, non-judgmental container in which to tenderly explore aspects that are raw, frightening, hidden, unknown, unconscious, or threatening to look at and open into. For McPhee, Presence includes giving ourselves totally or fully, which he says is the mark of intimacy (2005). Fully meeting open, available, and engaged is a kind of non-intrusive meeting and relating. As Lasley et al. (2011) says:

> Ironically, when we try to change people, they resist. In contrast, coaching helps people become more of who they already are. Simply witnessing the process and being fully present has a transformational impact. In holistic coaching we create an essence-to-essence relationship. (p. 6)

There have been many studies in various fields of nursing, hands on healing, Reiki, et cetera, that point to the impact one's presence has on his or her client or patient. Presence has significance in determining the quality of interpersonal contact (Rogers, 1961). It is evident that being fully present can have an astonishing impact on your interactions with clients.

Outside Time

"The constant iteration of letting go of a historical self, touching the present moment deeply, and allowing action to happen from here, shifts the idea of having a solid, stable identity" (Topp, 2006, p. 60).

Presence is outside the finite concept of time. In Reality, this moment is all there is. There is no pull to get somewhere else or to attain some other date and time. You can only ever experience the present moment, all else is simply thought taking you on a ball-and-chain journey into the memories of the past and the fantasies or worries of the future. It is quite disempowering to reside in thoughts of our interpretation of the past and our projections of the future. Mentally residing in time distracts from what is showing up now, and puts you in the quicksand of ever-changing mirages played in the mind. Meeting everything here for the first time, void of seeing through filters of past and future, is fresh and alive and completely unconfined. In *Nothing Personal*, Nirmala answers a question from a student:

> That's the truth, isn't it? You just don't know. You get angry enough to finally admit that you don't know. It's a bum deal that this Mystery that is so rich and so true doesn't give you a formula. Then all that is left to do is pay attention; everything else is useless. . . . what is present right now? What's left? (2007, p. 99)

Paying attention to what is here, what is showing up now, is all that is ever truly relevant.

Active Inquiry, Silent Stillness, and Practice:

1) *What does it feel like when someone is fully present with you?*

2) *What impact does their full presence have on your interaction with him or her?*

3) *How do you feel when you're in the presence of someone that is fully present?*

4) *What does it mean to be fully present with a client? Is it simply sharing physical space? Or is it something more, something a bit different?*

5) What might that look like?

Really meeting someone in the present moment is a sweet joining in the infinite timeless. It is uniting beyond all stories of the past and projections of the future, and be-ing with another from (as) the same source. We meet everything for the first time—fresh, right here. This is where true union resides, in the present moment beyond thoughts and stories of illusive dreams. If you never touch this alert, present moment, old tapes of cyclical conditioning will continue to run your life. All that has significance is appearing now. Picture a keen sense of attention, where you are too alert to what is happening, too alert to think. In Elizabeth Topp's dissertation, she shares:

> Presence, the ability to physically be with something and psychologically meet someone with no judgment or agenda, is often the healing agent that allows something to move out of a solid, fixed, unhealthy position and into an evolving shifting position. (2006, p. 53)

This healing agent of Presence begins to loosen and dissolve the stuck-ness of identifying with the fragile flotation of me as a solid and fixed person. This healing agent loosens the chains of bondage to this false identity that causes so much suffering. When we really "meet" each other here in spacious awareness, beyond all conceptual thought, we meet in the timeless essence; an ungraspable, formless dimension of Life itself.

In exploring presence, Topp takes a look at what both Senge et al. (2004) and Wilber (1979) say about what it means to be present, and whether that includes anything with past and future:

> Both Senge et al. and Wilber introduce the possibility of living in the present moment. However while Senge et al. opens the

present moment to include future possibilities, Wilber (1979) points out that attending to the future can also take us away from the present. Senge et al. seem interested in creating a future of new human possibility. In this way individuals must enter the present fully and move from here. Wilber and other existential and spiritual philosophers, whose priority is existential Truth-seeking over attaining a future vision of human possibility, risk diving even deeper into this moment, releasing themselves of the safety that comes from remaining psychologically connected to the next emerging moment. However, safety is not what Senge et al. allude to when they speak of this process as a cycle of constant death and rebirth. (2006, p. 60)

Many coaches highlight and focus on the importance and impact of developing future goals. Staying in the present and not jumping into the next emerging moment gives spaciousness, openness, and freedom for anything to arise without the filters of previous goals of what should be. Presence allows for fluid newness. Presence allows for changes to occur without being hooked on what was supposed to be. There is a freedom in moving from the present without the efforts to develop a future that is not here, and may never be.

Active Inquiry, Silent Stillness, and Practice:

1) *How does it feel to entertain the possible futility of creating and projecting future goals with yourself?*
2) *How does it feel to entertain the possible futility of creating and projecting future goals with your clients?*
3) *How might this change the way you interact with clients?*

Be still. Feel the quiet expanse of your existence. Move, see from, be here.

Yes to This—Noticing Acceptance

"What most people never do—is almost the last thing anyone does—is accept. No matter what the conditions. Really, truly, deeply accept. You'd be surprised what happens when you do this" (Dixon, 2012, p. 24).

Beyond the boundaries and identification with the personal self, freedom and total acceptance already exists. Noticing that acceptance is already here, is a sort of allowing of everything to be exactly the way it is. Resistance of this is futile. With this there is an ease in accepting everything that is showing up without the need to fix, change, or desire for it to be another way. Attempting to "fix" another is a subtle declaration that they are not okay the way they are right now. Deep acceptance is one of the most important and liberating practices of inquire one can sink into and offer ones' clients. Saying *Yes* to the innumerable ways humans express themselves, offers an okayness for clients to show up in full color. As C. C. Leigh says in *Becoming Divinely Human*, "experiencing your inner territory with full awareness of what you're encountering is the very act that will ultimately set you free" (2011, p. 47). This openness gives space to move out of destructive cycles and stuck-ness, and into a restful, free-flowing arena of open investigation.

Active Inquiry, Silent Stillness, and Practice:

1) *Let an issue arise that feels like a problem. When you are fully here, without entertaining the yesterdays and tomorrows, is there still a problem?*

2) *How might this feel to be in a place where everything is already allowed and nothing is resisted?*

3) *Can you recall an experience where there was an ease, an acceptance, even amidst a difficult external situation?*

4) *What happens when you allow everything to be as it is?*

5) *What am I not okay with in this moment?*

6) *What do I know that I don't want to know?*

7) *What occurs, what changes in your experience?*

8) *Is it really true?*

The present moment does not discriminate what is okay and what is not. It is all simply already allowed. Being fully present ends the internal war, the perception of separation between what should be and what actually is. The present also ends the search; the search for love, approval, worth, et cetera. Searching is a rejection of what is, and a projection of what is not yet or ought to be. In presence, there is no longer a feeling of needing this moment to be any different than the way it is. This is one of the definitions of suffering; desiring life to be other than what is here, now. Everything right here is exactly as it should be. Being present is the end of jumping from place to place in search for what is already here—in search for something other than this—other than who I really am. This however is not a *trying* to allow, that is just another form of separation; a me *trying* to accept. Everything is actually already accepted as it is prior to noticing.

Active Inquiry, Silent Stillness, and Practice:

1) *How might a client feel if he or she feels authentic freedom to truly be or say anything without his or her coach "trying" to accept?*

2) *What's it like to give space to everything that's here?*

3) *What's it like to give space to the thoughts and experiences that are present?*

4) *Is there room for all of it to be here without the interjection of pushing something away or pulling it closer?*

5) How freeing is it to give space to everything that arises?

6) When you give more and more space to everything, are you in your mind or are you noticing and seeing from your whole Being?

Offering this openness gives space to see how everything is already accepted. This Vast Space, Presence, is a fullness that can hold it all. It is an open spaciousness that can hold all the confusion, lack of clarity, frustration, suffering, and turmoil without the need to hide it, change it, or manipulate it. Imposing pressure to change tends to lock things into place even further. An unobtrusive welcoming allows for open movement and real freedom to emerge. Confusion, fear, frustration, et cetera needs a battle against it to continue. Allowing all of this to show forth—and sitting with it with conscious attention—gives space and opportunity to see and watch these cloud-like thoughts and sensations to move through. Notice any resistance to the moment, as this is where stuckness lives. As Jeff Foster says in *The Deepest Acceptance*:

> We want to control the ocean by managing the waves, so the waves that appear are only those we want to appear. All human suffering is a variation on this theme—trying to control the waves, trying to control our present-moment experience so it conforms to our ideas and concepts of how it should be. (2012, p. 56)

Being fully present allows attention to remain open to a greater field of awareness. This field of awareness contains an array of feelings, sensations, and circumstances that show up, some of which are not always desired, and thus often ignored or pushed away. The more we are able to see and embody spacious awareness and experience the spectrum of life as it is, the more we no longer find the need to avoid or repress aspects that show up, or seek means of mental or physical escape from what is actually here (Tart, 1994). Actions that rise out of this larger range of spaciousness, beyond suppression and denial, allow for clarity in action and response to situations (Epstein, 2003). Whatever is arising often has an important message. Being present and saying "yes" opens the floodgates to vulnerability and raw authenticity. Saying "yes" is an infinite freedom for all of life to show forth however it is arising, in all its' shapes and colors. Open listening offers freedom to experience this full range; the very gates that open to a vibrant aliveness that is so often sought.

Active Inquiry, Silent Stillness, and Practice:

1) *What if you (and your clients) could just be with it all, exactly as it is showing up right here in this moment?*

2) *How might a client feel if he/she feels freedom to truly be or say anything without his/her coach attempting to fix, change, rescue, or interject?*

Counseling, advising, fixing, and/or saving are all intrusive forms of external correction; all forms negating the okay-ness of how things are right now. Fixing someone or something gives the subtle message that something is not okay the way it is. It communicates that something is wrong and ought to be different, ought to change. This has the capacity to shut down ones capacity to stay open to deep inquiry and exploration of that which is currently unseen.

3) *Who would want to open up in total vulnerability, only to be imposed by subtle messages of "you need to change, you're not okay how you are, something's wrong with you"?*

4) *In your coaching sessions, is there spaciousness for anything to arise without the energy of pushing, pulling, changing, shutting someone down, or fixing?*

Tart (1994) shares a few "benefits" of being present with people (clients), explaining it:

> Can lead to a lot of moments of vividness, of beauty, of satisfaction, and of insight, as well as times when you have to stick in there and put up with awful realizations about yourself, embarrassing things, and clear perception of your own and others' cruelty and suffering. Gradually you develop a wider psychological space to live in a greater satisfaction in all areas of life. (p. 83)

Presence includes both awareness and attention, as it is open, focused, and alert (Colm, 1996; Craig, 1986).

Deep Listening

> We first thought of presence as being fully conscious and aware in the present moment. Then we began to appreciate presence as deep listening, of being open beyond one's pre-conceptions and historical ways of making sense. We came to see the importance of letting go of old identities and the need to control . . . Ultimately, we came to see all these aspects of presence as leading to a state of "letting come," of consciously participating in a larger field for change. (Senge et al., 2004, p. 11–12)

We all hear about listening in and around various coaching literature. Listen closely to clients, listen to the "still small voice," listen to your heart, listen inside, et cetera. But what does deep listening really mean? One of the most important aspects in looking deeply into this is in the recognition of where listening is really from. Is there a "someone" listening, hearing through the filtered lens of the thinking mind? Or is listening and hearing just happening?

Perhaps there is no "I" to even "do" the listening. Or is there a greater field where listening just happens?

Contact in Silence opens unobtrusive space to hear that which is not verbalized. Belf sums it up well in *Coaching with Spirit* when she says, "Listening occurs only in the present moment, and the power of listening is in silence" (2002, p. 59). There is great wisdom in the silence between words. McPhee agrees, sharing along these same lines, "Listening well involves silence" (2005, p. 16), it "involves determining the source and direction of the deeper currents below the surface" (p. 17). Sensitivity to these deeper currents requires a heightened sense of attentive awareness and quiet stillness. When there is quiet receptivity and awareness, it is possible to sense that which goes unsaid, but not unheard.

Active Inquiry, Silent Stillness, and Practice:

1) *Do you listen through the filters of the thinking mind?*
2) *Do you find a sense of ease and comfort in Silence?*
3) *Is there enough space for clients to just be still and inquire, process, and move at his or her own pace?*

Giving a client space—quiet silence—to investigate without jumping in and interjecting with an opinion, idea, interpretation, or avenue of escape from the present feeling, provides opportunity for him or her to sink in to the deeper layers of what is currently unconscious and driving the surface conditioning that is arising. Cutting off this inquiring space through imposing words of suggestions and ideas on how to fix or change, not only feels intrusive to a wide-open and vulnerable heart suggesting an inability to uncover one's own answers, but it also robs one of the opportunity to deeply investigate what is unconsciously deep below the surface.

Although deep, pointed questions and conversation can be incredibly supportive in a coaching environment, true depth does not necessarily come from words themselves. Listening deeply is graceful communion; it is absolutely central to authentic communication and deep connection. Listening deeply is central to really "hear" and feel into what another might be experiencing. Deep listening does not presume to know what others are really experiencing. However there is a sense of walking side-by-side, pulling in beside another, attentive to what is seen or what one may be experiencing. The deep interest to actually hear what another is feeling, experiencing, and hungering to express, opens up channels of union and communication which can sometimes otherwise be inhibited and shut down. Deep listening acknowledges another's present experience, without the need or desire to fix or change a thing.

In Silence, deep listening, acceptance, and compassion emerge. Conversation often slows, and there is space to relax and feel the underlying ground of peace amidst thought. When one feels heard and seen there is an offering to experience the still space of Silence. What greater gift than to offer a sweet space for another to be still, and recognize the complete all-ness of what's already here in the moment. Listening is quiet Love in action; a quiet Love that has immense power of deep connectivity.

Active Inquiry, Silent Stillness, and Practice:

1) *Do you offer clients unintrusive space to investigate the deeper layers arising within them?*

2) *What inhibits you to offer such space?*

Uncompromised Attention

The substance of space is recognized and experienced with uncompromised attention. Deep listening comes from Presence; undistracted, fully engaged, interested, and not caught up in the thoughts passing through the mind. As a coach, placing attention on the thinking mind that likes to plan, predict, strategize, and analyze is simply distraction from what is here. "Most of the time we appear to be focused on our internal dialogue and noise and do not pay attention to the speaker" (Belf, 2002, p. 59). Listening appears with quiet fascinated attention in the very freshness of the present moment. Attentive listening offers a renewed sense of wonder, awe, and curiosity; igniting clarity and vivid aliveness.

Active Inquiry, Silent Stillness, and Practice:

1) *Have you ever been talking with a friend and felt like they were just waiting for their turn to speak, not really listening at all?*

2) *What comes up for you with this interaction?*

3) *Have you ever been in conversation with a friend and felt his or her uncompromised, full attention, locked on you?*

4) *What comes up for you with this interaction?*

5) *Do you notice yourself preparing the next thing to say while your client is speaking?*

6) *Are you thinking about other things, distracted by the thoughts passing through, while your client is sharing?*

7) *Do you find yourself analyzing or strategizing while your client is speaking?*

8) *How might things be different if you were not entertaining these thoughts while listening?*

Listening Is Seen Connection

Listening is simultaneously seeing oneself and another. As touched on in an earlier chapter, what is seen is often significantly more important than what is said. What one sees is what is often communicated and subtly felt, regardless of verbal exchange. The gift to be heard, seen, felt, and cared for from infinite connectedness is a transformative offering. Listening deeply invites authentic connection and communion, breaking barriers of perceived differences and dividedness. This togetherness, rather than differentiated, divided, or hierarchical filtered way of seeing and operating, unites rather than creating gaps and division. Without this deep basis of listening, the speaker can often be left feeling unheard, unseen, unknown, and misunderstood.

Active Inquiry, Silent Stillness, and Practice:

1) *Have you ever been talking with a friend and felt like their eyes just penetrate through your whole system . . . as if they see you deep inside?*

2) *What comes up for you with this interaction?*

3) *Have you ever felt like someone is listening to you from a place of division rather than connectedness?*

4) *What, if any, signs and signals do you notice when this is taking place?*

5) *What comes up for you with this interaction?*

6) *What do you notice with clients when listening is happening from this undivided, seen connection?*

Listening Evokes Raw Honesty, Inquiry, and Fresh Aliveness

This listening/seeing invites one to hear, notice, and see for themselves beyond the drama of their story. Deep, truthful listening invites honesty—what is really here—to show forth without the fear of rejection, shame, or embarrassment to be unwelcomed and/or dismissed. Deep listening allows space for raw vulnerability to come forth out of hiding. An honest listener wants nothing more than for the other person to speak their raw truth, without fear of response or a feeling of what should be said, or what is acceptable or not. Clarity is often experienced when given such space to self-explore, inquire, and share without interruption, interpretation, personal opinion, or interjected experience. Raw honesty makes things clear, leaving little room for misunderstanding and misinterpretation. McPhee (2005) shares, "Here inner-knowing is introduced as a form of knowledge that can contribute to a deeper understanding and clarity of what is happening from moment to moment" (p. 16). Deep listening offers patient space for the speaker to be still and inquire, to see what is really being experienced in the moment, and to share with raw authenticity. This opening up gives space to unravel stories and see ones' own stuck-ness—and one's own solutions—clarifying action. When given this space to inquire, there is an indescribable freedom and sense of aliveness that abounds. True transformation takes place when clients are seen, and have room to fully be who they are.

Deep listening invites one to be completely engaged, fully alive, and tapped in to the vibrancy and connectedness of Life. Interaction void of this depth of listening has the power to disengage, inhibit, and squelch. Listening deeply provides space for the birth of new ideas; the willingness to be wide open to newness and insight.

When people feel seen and heard, they often become fully present, fully engaged, and fully alive.

Active Inquiry, Silent Stillness, and Practice:

1) *What fears come up for you in your own inquiry in questioning the stories of who you are?*

2) *Do you give yourself space to just be still, inquire, and process without judgment?*

3) *What do you notice or experience when you engage in conversations of raw honesty?*

4) *Do you offer clients unintrusive space to investigate the deeper layers arising within them?*

5) *What fears arise in offering clients full space to explore the raw truth of what's showing up for them?*

6) *In what ways might you not be open to your clients fully expressing and sharing? Are you open to it all?*

7) *How might these ways squelch your sessions?*

5 RADICAL SINCERITY

The capacity and willingness to be honest with yourself is your greatest guard against self-deception and deceit, and aligns you with your genuine aspiration.

There is no greater challenge for a human being than to be completely honest with oneself as well as with others, and yet such honesty is absolutely necessary if we are ever to awaken to our dream of separation and live a truly genuine and undivided life. (Adyashanti, 2012a, p. 6)

Dropping into your heart-space (the whole of Being) and out of your head is the first step to sincerely relating and meeting authentically. If you are in your head, you cannot sincerely join with another. Sincerely joining with another requires you to drop out of the personal me borders where thoughts, judgments, opinions, et cetera reside and to open into the depths of who or what you really are. Opening into Essence, or sinking deeper through self, and into your heart-space and feeling ones' expansiveness, gives way to genuine sincerity.

Agenda

One sure-fire way to lose touch with sincerity is to come in with an agenda—any agenda. As a coach, are you moving from a place through the filter of seeking approval, love, or appreciation? Or are you perhaps operating from the feeling that you need the client financially, or for your own healing process or desires? When moving from any needing/seeking place, actions shift, and authentic connection is skewed. There is no longer a clean attentiveness, but movement filtered through passive intent and desire. As Jeff Foster says in *The Deepest Acceptance*:

> To put it simply, as long as you are seeking, you are always playing a little game with them and with yourself, even if you don't realize it. You are secretly adapting your behavior, changing what you say, hiding what you really feel, being careful, in order to ensure that they keep giving you what you want. . . ,You start performing, rather than relating. You relate as an image to another image, rather than as open space to open space—and your relationships can end up feeling totally incomplete and unsatisfying. (2012, p. 168)

Active Inquiry, Silent Stillness, and Practice:

1) *Do you have any subtle, hidden agenda or intention in any of your sessions?*

2) *Do you desire your clients to stop struggling and wish they would be happy and successful?*

3) *Is there anything you want from your client right now? (Example: I want to be understood, liked, appreciated . . .)*

   Another form of agenda is in leading questions.

4) *Do you use questions to lead or steer clients in a particular direction?*

5) *Are your questions suggestive or subtly coercive to a particular response, laced with intention or desired outcome (be it through question structure, wording, tone, etc.)?*

6) *Or, do you actually give space and really not know, seeing they are actually the only knower?*

"In the magic something state, there are no rules or inhibitions or calculated maneuvers" (Dixon, 2012, p. 11). In this "magic something state," as Dixon calls it, there is room to let anything and everything arise that needs to surface. Being in the unknown and being/offering this porous space, allows anything to freely surface without judgment. Clients have all of the answers they need.

Active Inquiry, Silent Stillness, and Practice:

1) *If it is true that clients have all the answers they need, how might you show up differently in your sessions with clients?*

2) *Is it possible to simply let Life emerge in the way it wants to emerge without unnecessarily interfering or paving a particular path?*

Holding this space is quite boundary-less, open, and vast—spacious enough for anything to show up that needs to show up—providing an environment conducive to unexpected openings, newness, and expansiveness. Being comfortable in not having a plan and in authentically not knowing, gives space for clients to sincerely explore. A "don't know" curiosity cultivates openness into what has not been seen, and shines the light on untouched, vulnerable, and hidden blocks. Giving space to sincerely explore provides opportunity to genuinely look into and see through the illusions, games, and ways of escape that have been used to avoid what is really here. Supporting an agenda-less "unknown" space for clients to also not know and look with innocent curiosity and open-newness to unforeseen possibilities, gives spaciousness for clarity to rise and liberation to be experienced.

Active Inquiry, Silent Stillness, and Practice:

1) *Are you comfortable not having a plan and giving space for anything to show up in client sessions?*

2) *Do you notice any need to control with a plan?*

3) *What fears come up for you when you feel into letting go of the need to control with a plan?*

4) *What might it look like to be in this "agenda-less unknown" space with a client?*

Authenticity—Pulling In

Entering into the world of the client and deeply meeting him or her in his or her world of perception is one of the most kind, gentle, unimposing means to pull in beside someone's journey and really "be" with him or her with great authenticity. Without getting caught up in the story, enter in, and walk through the very fields of challenges, suffering, contemplation, joy et cetera; simply listening, feeling, and seeing his or her experience the way he or she may be experiencing in the moment, finding that place that connects and is true for you, and allowing their experience to be yours. This bridges the gap between speaker and listener. Seeing eye-to-eye, relating, and feeling from the gritty humanness that is present with all humans, is authentic, honest connection. Seeing through and embracing all stories—simply joining in the passenger seat looking side-by-side and feeling as humans feel—honors the great intelligence at play. Simply walk beside, without things needing to change, without the need to give advice, and without the need to fix anything. It is here you will meet a sweet truth, a deep sincerity, a rawness of authentic present-moment experience. Wearing your clients' shoes, walking on their path—seeing, hearing, and experiencing from their current perspective—is where you authentically meet. This is where you find all aspects, in all shapes of life, within every human being. When meeting in this way, deep compassion and tender sincerity can seep from your very being and touch others with the sweetest intimacy, care, and genuine heart. This genuine meeting of entering in and walking together beyond all agenda and story, breeds compassion, love, healing, and connectivity beyond words.

Active Inquiry, Silent Stillness, and Practice:

1) *How do you listen with authenticity, offering raw openness to freely share?*

2) *How do you pull in beside your clients without getting swept into the stories?*

Masks of Persona

An experience of authentic being is described as an experience of no façade, no roles or pretense, and no censoring (Kokinakis, 1995; Rogers, 1961). When one is "fully aware of oneself" (Kokinakis, 1995, p. 116), recognizing all the ways we slip back into identification with the self, the more transparent and authentic we are with clients. "When one can simply be him or herself, or be authentic, then no content of experience needs to be rejected or denied. Therefore all of one's attention may remain present within the larger field of awareness" (Topp, 2006, p. 57). As a coach, self-awareness is key to authenticity. The more masks you wear, the less authentically you behave. The less identified you are with these masks of persona, the more alert you will be to all of the ways one is magnetically pulled back into the agenda of the mind. Authenticity with oneself is the crux of being authentic with someone else. Do not play the coach, the therapist, the healer, the savior, the nice guy or the one who can help or the one who knows. These roles/personas are unfortunately quite common in most every day relationships, and can be quite detrimental in the coach-client relationship.

Active Inquiry, Silent Stillness, and Practice:

1) *What persona's do you play in your role as a coach?*
2) *What masks to you portray and wear, hiding to shield from total exposure?*
3) *What fears do you have in releasing these masks?*
4) *What do you get by wearing these masks? (to feel safe, to feel smart, to feel loved, to feel separate, etc.)?*

Realness

Be fully human. Being fully human with clients, without filtering what you think you should or should not be or do, also sets the stage for your clients to do and be themselves 100% without masks and smoke screens of images and personas. Your authentic realness invites clients to open into being completely real as well. The freedom to be oneself, wholly and authentically, is not often fully embraced in our society, and yet authenticity is what brings clarity and healing, which is what so many humans crave. Realness is honest; it is not hiding behind the need to solicit anything from the other person. This kind of sincerity is where true connection takes place. In deep sincerity, clients are invited to be real, to open, and to be free to genuinely explore. It fascinates me to hear how many coaches feel a need to be seen as perfect, flawless, or at least present themselves as completely put together and having it all figured out since they are the coach. This misperception of needing to have it all figured out, to be perfect, or to have your life look a certain way, can ironically act as the very barrier to sincere connection with clients. Let clients see your humanity, the grittiness of all human beings. Coaches, therapists, teachers, et cetera do not need to have mastered life to be an incredible coach. Life cannot be mastered. Life is messy, regardless of the chosen profession. Being with another in a raw, human way with all the humanness life brings about is a refreshing, beautiful offering of realness. It invites clients to simply be human, in the full spectrum of human qualities and expression.

Active Inquiry, Silent Stillness, and Practice:

1) *Are you authentically real and sincere with your clients?*
2) *Do you need your clients to see you in a particular way?*
3) *What insecurities arise in letting these "needed" images fade away?*
4) *What do you get by not being fully real and authentic?*
5) *Do any fears arise in meeting clients in this real way?*

Honesty—Fire of Grace

Authenticity contains a fire of truth, a sort of fierce grace. This authenticity supports and evokes truth and deep honesty. Honesty is the greatest means to avoid the attempt to deceive oneself. Honesty is a willingness to stop trying to trick oneself, and actually take a look and really see what is present. Living from, and coaching from, a fire of truth can certainly be felt by clients. Truth can sometimes be felt like an intense fire, burning through to the core of what is really true. It can sometimes leave a client feeling naked to the shock of present reality, unable to hide and continue to self-deceive. Although this fire can feel hot, this depth of honesty is Love, and liberates. However it does not sugar-coat:

> When you have everything you're ever going to want right in the moment, you have nothing to lose or hide or cover up, and open-eyed honesty just naturally arises. There is no agenda and no fear. This may sound pedantic, but trust me it's not. Human interaction on this level is an astonishing element of living with 'magic something.' (Dixon, 2012, p. 8)

Active Inquiry, Silent Stillness, and Practice:

1) *In what ways do you avoid deep honesty with yourself?*

2) *In what ways do you avoid deep honesty with your clients?*

3) *In what ways to you skirt a topic or a confrontation with your clients?*

4) *Are you okay asking "honest, fierce grace" questions to your clients that may make them uncomfortable, irritated, angry, et cetera.?*

5) *Can you recall a scenario where you chose not to ask a question out of fear of the clients' response?*

6) *Can you see how your own fear to inquire from this deep honesty can compromise your clients' capacity to touch freedom?*

6 TRUSTING LIFE

"The Truth is revealed when we allow ourselves to not know, so I invite you to set aside all that you know for the time being and allow yourself to look with innocent eyes" (Nirmala, 2007, unnumbered).

Knowing in Not Knowing

There is an underlying "knowing"—conscious or not—that Life always takes care of itself. Recognition of this brings about a natural resting. This resting is the release of identification with this separate me that needs to figure things out. As C. C. Leigh says in *Becoming Divinely Human*, "You don't have to figure this all out—any more than you have to tell your heart to beat" (2011, p. 51). Coming from this is invigorating and empowering in a coach-client relationship. Moving from this space allows clients to learn to trust the truth within, and not depend on any external source(s) for their own clarity and knowing. When coaches act like they know something that the client does not know about him or herself, it is disempowering, and teaches the client to distrust themselves, and lean on and seek answers outside themselves.

Active Inquiry, Silent Stillness, and Practice:

1. *Is there anything we really know for sure about what our clients need?*

2. *Can we really know what is necessary for our clients in the moment or even the next moment?*

3. *How might your sessions change with this clarity? What might change with you? What might change with your client(s)?*

Perhaps the only thing we really know is that none of us really know anything. The forever unknown gives a raw aliveness that meets what is needed in each and every moment. The moment we think we know something, is the moment we are lost in thoughts of the chattering mind. When caught in this clutter, there can be a feeling of disconnect from the deep wisdom that naturally unfolds. Within (each) Being lies truth, wisdom, non-division, and clarity. "When you finally admit that you don't know anything, that's when you start paying attention" (Nirmala, 2007, p. 22).

Walls of Certainty

Earlier in the section entitled, Density and Transparency with Clients, we talked about how clients can bump into believed concepts as who I am in his or her coach. As the coach, when you are identified with the stories of me, you are bound to have many held beliefs you are really certain about. When you are certain about something (verbally expressed or not), these certainties can be felt like a rigid barrier. When someone is certain, there is no longer a welcomed openness to explore any other possibilities. Why would there be an openness if someone were certain of how something is? When clients bump into certainties in you, conscious or unconscious, there can be felt blockage(s) in the interaction, inhibiting one to freely explore and investigate. Whatever the topic, when someone is certain it becomes closed and known, and not open for unattached, exploratory discussion. In *Nothing Personal*, Nirmala shares, "The Truth is revealed when we allow ourselves to not know, so I invite you to set aside all that you know for the time being and allow yourself to look with innocent eyes" (2007, unnumbered). The only place you can really connect with your clients with innocent eyes is in a place of open uncertainty. In open uncertainty there is an unknown newness in every moment with child-like curiosity to discover what is possibly here. Uncertainty is actually reality. There is a vibrant, extraordinariness (and ordinariness) in the unknown.

In *The Shift*, Wayne Dyer says, "What was true in the morning has become a lie in the afternoon" (2009). So what we have learned to be true in one instance may not be true or relevant in another. Each moment is fresh, new, and relevant to this here, not necessarily the same as that which was relevant before. Each moment calls for something different, unexpected, and unknown until it arises. If we hold in thought that which ought to work, should be helpful since it was before, worked last week, was learned in a book and was successful, et cetera, it is not only stale and perhaps not accurate, but we are no longer fully present with the client while lost in thoughts, preconceived notions, and old conclusions. Certainty is the end of curiosity, broad possibility, and openness to what is really, fully here.

Have you ever been in conversation with someone that has an opinion and knowing about everything? It makes it quite challenging to relate deeply to someone when there are layers upon layers of built up beliefs, opinions, judgments, and impenetrable ideas creating barriers to authentic connection. Eckhart Tolle, in *The Power of Now,* sums it up well when he states:

> Identification with your mind creates an opaque screen of concepts, labels, images, words, judgments, and definitions that blocks all true relationship. It comes between you and yourself, between you and your fellow man and woman, between you and nature, between you and God. (1999, p. 15)

Active Inquiry, Silent Stillness, and Practice:

1) *Do you offer this unknown openness, this spaciousness, to your clients?*

2) *What is the thickness, the density of layered certainty that you bring into your interactions with your clients?*

3) *How solid are the layers and grooves of certainties, of conditioning and identification with the personal "I," the separate me?*

4) *What do you believe to be true (walls of certainty), that might not actually be real, that clients may pick up on?*

5) *What are you certain about that may shut down inquiry and expansive possibility?*

6) *These blockages, beliefs, and opinions; how might they affect your clients, consciously and unconsciously? I invite you to investigate.*

These thick, belief structures have the potential to create a heavy barrier between you and your clients, and are quite possibly worth looking into. When there is spaciousness and transparency, there is a liberating invitation to walk into this free-flowing, open meadow, where everything is up for question and investigation and nothing is for certain. How liberating and connective!

Non-Reliance

Eventually clients will need less and less from their time with you. As clients begin to trust all the communication that is coming from within, questions will naturally answer themselves and there will not be such a need to have the coach mirror back his or her own truth. Clients actually know the answer(s) to their questions, otherwise they would not be asking. Formulating the question has the answer right within the construction of the inquiry. So rather than answering questions, simply question answers. Holding space and simply raising up a mirror is all that is often necessary. How liberating to release all responsibility to be the one who needs to know, needs to help, needs to do anything.

Active Inquiry, Silent Stillness, and Practice:

1) *Silence truly is the deepest teacher, and holds the greatest wisdom. If this is true, how might you show up in this space with your clients?*

2) *In what ways, be it through speech or action, might you be creating a coach/client interaction that is laced with reliance?*

3) *If you do notice your client continually reliant on you, how might you continuously turn it back, reminding him or her of their own knowingness?*

The ground of being is a significant fundamental ingredient missing in current coaching literature. This missing ingredient—and the elements that ensue—gives evident rise for a new model to be deeply explored. Moving from the common self-development phenomena, to a foundation in the timeless dimension of being and seeing, will offer a deeply transformative way in which coaching can take place.

CONCLUSION

Transformation happens when people are seen as the Essence of who they truly are. A fundamental shift in identification, from the conceptual, mind-generated personal self, to the ground of being, has the capacity to expand transformative possibilities of the coaching client as well as the field of coaching. This ground of being is a significant fundamental ingredient currently lacking in coaching literature. The ground of being—and the elements that permeate this Essence—gives evident rise for a new model to be deeply explored. Shifting from the popular self-development movement, to a foundation in the timeless dimension of being and seeing, will offer a deeply transformative way in which coaching can take place. Although this model is not something that can be "learned" over a given period of time like a typical skill-set, it can serve as a foundation with hopes to provide a springboard in which to ignite an interest in further discovery.

POTENTIAL BARRIERS

The concepts introduced and explored ask the coach to question and examine him or herself on a deep level, challenging ones' current set of ideas, beliefs, concepts, and perceived personal identity in a way that might not feel all that comfortable. It is understandable that not every coach will be up for the task and challenge to deeply explore and examine oneself and his or her "stuff." Some may not be up for this internal inquiry, nor interested in the potential power it can have to dramatically alter one's sense of self, and one's coaching practice.

The language used often points to the intangible; that which exists beyond the thinking mind, skill-sets, and avenues of logical knowledge. This is not necessarily easy to understand, but asks one to explore, feel, and directly experience beyond the comprehension and logic of the educated, academic mind.

Some physicians, coaches, and therapists in this role may have a challenging time allowing for an equal environment—or "playing field"—between themselves and their client/patients. Many individuals in the coaching profession have a strong need to be the one in authority. This can rub against one's ability to have an interest in or desire the recognition of equality and sameness in the coach/client relationship. This may serve as a barrier to the receptivity of this new model.

Coming into the "I don't know" mentality may be a challenge for most any coach audience. There is a heavy influence for more, more, more; be it higher education, skill-sets, strategies, techniques, knowledge, experience, et cetera. Rarely is it encouraged that a deeper knowing may contain the most powerful aspect to open into and see that's all that is often necessary. The coaching role is often perceived as being the one that knows, and will guide you down your path and point you in the right direction. Setting aside all notions of the one that knows or one that ought to know can be quite liberating. Although liberating, it releases this sense of control, which may not be something every coach will be willing or interested to explore.

Unlike learning a traditional, learned skill, these elements are not typically ones that are simply read, retained, perfected, and completed like an academic text. Conversely, these elements are felt, seen, and deeply known like seeds that germinate and sprout into a fresh seeing, clearer realization; shifting in action as expression and reflection. Understanding concepts through studying, learning, and intellectual expansion holds a different texture than the seeing through and dissolving of old belief structures as a means of clearer congruency with the elements of this new model. Closing the gap between learning a new skill set and putting it into practice has a different quality from the implementation of this new model and really seeing and experiencing firs- hand what the words are pointing to.

The rate of the coaches' evolution is in direct relation and proportion to which this work will be authentically "applicable" to the coaches' practice.

REFERENCES

Adyashanti. (2006). *True meditation.* Boulder, CO: Sounds True..

Adyashanti. (2011). *Falling into grace: Insights on the end of suffering.* Boulder, CO: Sounds True.

Adyashanti. (2012a). *The way of liberation.* Campbell, CA: Open Gate Sangha, Inc.

Adyashanti. (2012b) *The way of liberation – Self-guided study course* [CD]. Campbell, CA: Open Gate Sangha, Inc.

Adyashanti. (2012c). *The immensity of solitude.* Retrieved from http://www.adyashanti.org/index.php?file=writings_inner&writingid=52

Amazon. (2013) *Dying into this.* Retrieved from http://www.amazon.com/Dying-Into-This-Prajna-Ana/dp/1480041947

Ana, P. (2013). *Dying into this.* Retrieved from http://www.amazon.com/Dying-Into-This-Prajna-Ana/dp/1480041947/ref=sr_1_1?ie=UTF8&qid=1357064628&sr=8-1&keywords=Dying+Into+This

Askew, S, & Carnell, E. (2011). *Transformative coaching: A learning theory for practice.* London: Institute of Education, University of London.

Belf, T. (2002). *Coaching with spirit: Allowing success to emerge.* San Francisco: Jossey-Bass/Pfeiffer.

Bergo, B. (2005). *Emmanuel Levinas: Critical assessments of leading philosophers.* New York: Routledge.

Boadella, D. (1998).Essence and ground: Towards the understanding of spirituality in psychotherapy. *International Journal of Psychotherapy, 3*(1), 29–51.

Bryson, K. (2004). *Don't be nice, be real.* Santa Rosa, CA: Elite Books.

Cashman, K. (1998). *Leadership from the inside out: Becoming a leader for life.* Provo, UT: Executive Excellence.

Colm, H. (1996). *The existential approach to psychotherapy with adults and children.* New York: Grune & Stratton.

Craig, E. (1986). Sanctuary and presence: An existential view of the therapist's contribution. *Humanistic Psychologist, 14*, 22–28.

Csikszentmihalyi, M. (2000). *Beyond boredom and anxiety.* San Francisco: Jossey-Bass/Pfeiffer.

Csikszentmihalyi, M,, & Larson, R. (1978). Intrinsic rewards in school crime. *Crime and Delinquency, 24*, 322–335.

Dixon, S. (2012). *21 days, A guide for spiritual beginners: The gritty rarely revealed.* Charlottesville, VA: PIE Publishing.

Dyer, W. (Director/Performer). (2009). *The shift* [DVD]. Carlsbad, CA: Hay House.

Einstein, A. (2013). Retrieved from http://www.goodreads.com/quotes/16479-once-you-can-accept-the-universe-as-matter-expanding-into

Epstein, R. M. (2003). Mindful practice in action: Technical competence, evidence-based medicine, and relationship-centered care. *Families, Systems, & Health 21*, 1–9.

Evered, R., &Selman, J. (1987). Coaching and the art of management. *Organizational Dynamics, 18*, 16–32.

Forman, K. C. (1998). *The innate capacity: Mysticism, philosophy and psychology.* New York, Oxford: Oxford University Press.

Foster, J. (2012). *The deepest acceptance; Radical awakening in ordinary life.* Boulder, CO: Sounds True.

Frydman, M., & Dikshit, S. S (1999). *I am that: Talks with Sri Nisargadatta Maharaj.* Durham, NC: Acorn Press.

Gangaji. (2007). *You Are That.* Boulder, CO: Sounds True.

Gangaji. (2009). Just stop [video]. *Retrieved from http://www.youtube.com/watch?v=P-wX7KWOYGs*

Gangaji. (2011). *Hidden treasure.* New York: Penguin Group.

Greenblatt, M. (2002); *The essential teachings of Ramana Maharshi: A visual journey.* Vista, CA: Inner Directions.

Grof, S. (2007). Holotropic experiences and their healing and heuristic potential. Retrieved from http://www.stanislavgrof.com/pdf/Psychology%20of%20the%20 Future.pdf

Grof, S. (2008). A brief history of transpersonal psychology. Retrieved from http://www.stanislavgrof.com/pdf/A%20Brief%20History%20of %20Transpersonal%20Psychology-Grof.pdf

Grof, S. (2013). Revision and re-enchantment of psychology: legacy from half century of consciousness reearch [video]. Retrieved from http://www.scienceandnonduality.com/thankyou-livestream.shtml

Hargrove, R. (1999). *Masterful coaching.* San Francisco: Jossey-Bass/Pfeiffer.

Hart, T., Nelson, P.L.,Puhakka, K. (2000). *Transpersonal knowing: Exploring the horizon of consciousness.* Albany, NY: State University of New York Press.

Hyde, B. (1995). An ontological approach to education. Paper presented at the Annual Meeting of the Western States Communication Association, Portland, OR.

Johnson, R., & Eaton, J. (2001). *Coaching successfully*. New York: Dorling Kindersley Pub,.

Katie, B. (2013). About the work. Retrieved from http://www.thework.com/thework.php

Kokinakis, C. L. (1995). Teaching professional standards: Training yoga therapists in loving presence. *Dissertation Abstract International, 57*(2A), 588. (UMI No. AAM9619848).

Laske, O. E. (2003). *An integrated model of developmental coaching: Researching new ways of coaching and coach education.* Denver, CO: Paw Print Press.

Lasley, M. (2010). *Facilitating with heart: Awakening personal transformation and social change.* Troy, PA: Lulu Press.

Lasley, M., Kellogg, V., Michaels, R. & Brown, S. (2011). *Coaching for transformation: Pathways to ignite personal and social change.* Troy, PA: Discover Press.

Leigh, C. C. (2011). *Becoming divinely human.* Portland, OR: Wolfsong Press.

Levinas, E. (1969). *Totality and infinity: An essay on exteriority.* Pittsburgh, PA: Dequesne University Press.

Long, D. (2011). *Body knowledge: A path to wholeness.* Bloomington, IN: Xlibris Corporation.

Maslow, A. H. (1968). *Toward a psychology of being.* New York: Van Nostrand Reinhold.

Masters, R. (2010). *Spiritual bypassing: When spirituality disconnects us from what really matters.* Berkeley, CA: North Atlantic Books.

McPhee, S. J. (2005, April 6). The practice of presence. Presentation given at the Palliative Care Service and Palliative Care Leadership Center at the University of California, San Francisco, CA.

Mitchell, S. (1998). *Tao te ching; Anew English version.* New York: Harper Collins Publishers.

Mooji. (2011).Reaction of Anger to Unfairness [video]. Retrieved from https://www.youtube.com/watch?v=LIoCw5zy6I4

Mooji. (2013). What is Awakening? [video]. Retrieved from https://www.youtube.com/watch?v=t2P-2PLfyTY

Neill, M. (2011). Retrieved from http://www.supercoach.com/weekly/mnct773.shtml

Nhat Hahn, Thich. (1995). *Living Buddha, Living Christ.* New York: Riverhead Books.

Nirmala. (2007). Nothing personal: Seeing beyond the illusion of a separate self. Retrieved from http://endless-satsang.com: Endless Satsang Foundation

Nirmala. (2008) *Living from the heart.* Sedona, AZ: Endless Satsang Foundation.

Osteen, J. (2007). *Become a better you.* New York: Free Press.

Richards, K. (2013). Facebook entry. Retrieved from https://www.facebook.com/pages/Karen-Richards/189872017705672?fref=ts

Rogers, C. (1961). *On becoming a person.* Boston: Houghton Mifflin.

Rothberg, D. (1994). Spiritual inquiry. *Revision, 17*(2), 2–12.

Schaik, V. (2012). *Create yourself: Claim yourself and consciously create yourself.* South Africa: Liquid Edge Publishing.

Seligman, M. E. P. (2002). *Positive psychology, positive prevention, and positive therapy.* New York: Oxford University Press.

Senge, P., Jaworski, C. O., & Flowers, B. S. (2004).*Presence: Human purpose and the field of the future*. Cambridge, MA: Society for Organizational Learning.

Silsbee, D. (2008). *Presence-based coaching: Cultivating self-generative leaders through mind, body, and heart*, 1st ed. San Francisco: Jossey-Bass.

Stephens, W. (1972). *Life in the open sea*. NewYork: McGraw-Hill.

Tart, C. T. (1994). *Living the mindful life*. Boston: Shambhala.

Tolle, E. (1999). *The power of now: A guide to spiritual enlightenment*. Novato, CA: New World Library.

Topp, E. (2006). Presence-based coaching: The practice of presence in relation to goal-directed activity. Unpublished doctoral dissertation, Institute of Transpersonal Psychology, Palo Alto, CA.

Valle, R. S, King, M., & Halling, S. (1989). *Existential-phenomenological perspectives in psychology*. New York: Plenum Press.

Wade, J. (1996). *Changes of mind a holonomic theory of the evolution of consciousness*. Albany, NY: State University of New York Press.

Watts, A. (1975). *Tao: The watercourse way*. New York: Pantheon Books.

Welwood, J. (2000). *Toward a psychology of awakening: Buddhism, psychotherapy, and the path of personal and spiritual transformation*. Boston: Shambhala.

Wilber, K. (1979). *No boundry*. Boston: Shambhala.

Wilber, K. (2000). *Integral psychology*. Boston: Shambhala.

Wilber, K. (2004). *The simple feeling of being: Embracing your true nature*. Boston: Shambhala.

Wilber, K. (2007). Ken Wilber – I Am Big Mind [video]. Retrieved from *https://www.youtube.com/watch?v=BA8tDzK_kPI*

Williamson, M. (2008). *Inagural Speech*. Retrieved from

http://www.lmsf.mq.edu.au/LMSF_docs/wmer_docs/wmer200
8/papers/standup_nelsonmandela.pdf

APPENDIX A

Other Supportive Literature

Adyashanti. (2006). *Emptiness dancing*, 2nd ed. Boulder, CO: Sounds True.

Berland, W. (1999). *Out of the box for life: Being free is just a choice.* New York: HarperCollins Publishers.

Carter-Scott, C. (2007). *Transformational life coaching: Creating limitless opportunities for yourself and others.* Deerfield Beach, FL: Health Communications, Inc.

Corey, G. (1996). *Theory and practice of counseling and psychotherapy.* Pacific Grove, CA: Brooks/Cole.

Covey, S. (2003). *The 7 habits of highly effective people personal workbook.* New York: Simon & Schuster.

Dyer, W. (2004). *The power of intention: Learning to co-create your world your way.* Carlsbad, CA: Hay House.

Epstein, R. M. (2001, January). Just Being. *The Western Journal of Medicine, 174*(1), 63–65.

Flaherty, J. (1999). *Coaching: Evoking excellence in others.* Boston: Butterworth Heinemann.

Goleman, D. (1997). *Emotional intelligence.* New York: Bantam Books.

Hayward, J. (1998). A Rdzogs-chen Buddhist interpretation of the sense of self. *Journal of Consciousness Studies,* 5(5–6), 611–626.

Heeter, C. (1992). The subjective experience of presence. *Presence, 1*(2), 262–271.

Hendricks, G., &. Hendricks, K. (1993). *At the speed of life: A new approach to personal change through body-centered therapy.* New York: Bantam Books.

Jourard, S. M. (1971). *The transparent self.* New York: Van Nostrand Reinhold.

Kane, A., & Kane, S. (2009).*Working on yourself doesn't work:The 3 simple ideas that will instantaneously transform your life.* New York: McGraw-Hill.

Katie, B., & Mitchell, S. (2002). *Loving what is: Four questions that can change your life.* New York: Harmony Books.

Krieger, D. (1993). *Accepting your power to heal: The personal practice of therapeutic touch.* Santa Fe, NM: Bear.

Lake, G. (2007). *Radical happiness: A guide to awakening,* 2nd ed. Sedona, AZ: Endless Satsang Foundation.

Loy, D. (1983). How many nondualities are there. *Journal of Indian Philosophy, 11,* 413–426.

Frankl, V. (1997). *Man's search for meaning.* London: Pocket Books.

Nakamura, J, & Csikszentmihalyi, M. (2002). *The concepts of flow.* New York: Oxford University Press.

Palmer, P. (2000). *Let your life speak: Listening for the voice of vocation.* San Francisco: Jossey-Bass.

Palmer, P. (2004). *A hidden wholeness: The journey toward an undivided life: Welcoming the soul and weaving community in a wounded world.* San Francisco: Jossey-Bass.

Pressfield, S. (2002). *The war of art: Break through the blocks and win your inner creative battles.* New York: Warner Books.

Ray, R. (2008). *Touching enlightenment: Finding realization in the body.* Boulder, CO: Sounds True.

Ruiz, M. *The four agreements: A practical guide to personal freedom.* San Rafael, CA: Amber-Allen Pub..

Sieler, A. (2003). *Coaching to the human soul: Ontological coaching and deep change.* Melbourne, Australia: Newfield Institute.

Singer, M. (2007). *The untethered soul: The journey beyond yourself.* Oakland, CA: New Harbinger Publications.

Wilber, K. (2008). *Integral life practice: A 21st century blueprint for physical health, emotional balance, mental clarity, and spiritual awakening.* Boston: Integral Books.

Williams, P., & Davis, D. (2002). *Therapist as life coach: Transforming your practice.* New York: W.W. Norton.

Williams, P., & Thomas, L. (2005). *Total life coaching: 50+ life lessons, skills & techniques to enhance your practice—and your life!* New York: W.W. Norton & Co.

Wyndham, J. (1994). *The ultimate freedom.* Long Beach, CA: Mountaintop Pub.

ABOUT THE AUTHOR

Carole Griggs received her Doctorate degree in Professional Coaching and Human Development in 2013 from International University of Professional Studies. She received her MA in Education; Teaching from Alliant International University in 2009, and completed her BA in Geography in 2001 from Eastern Illinois University. Carole is CHEK Coach Certified (Corrective Holistic Exercise Kinesiology), is a Certified Nutritionist (CMTA), and is Reiki II certified.

Carole is currently founder and CEO of **Open to Life.** She is an Integral Life Coach and Holistic Wellness Practitioner, currently practicing in San Diego, California, and traveling nationally and internationally. Carole is also an educational consultant with Houghton Mifflin Harcourt, providing professional development workshops to K-12 school districts throughout the US, and developing curriculum and standard courses for public school systems nationwide.

Carole has been in professional coaching and teaching since 2001, starting her career off as a middle school teacher at a charter school in San Diego, helping the school open during its beginning days in 2003. After classroom teaching, Carole started Empowering Fitness, a holistic health and wellness company, working with clients of all ages and stages of life throughout southern California. In 2011, Carole began Open to Life, a Life Coaching and Holistic Wellness practice that operates nationwide, based in San Diego, California.